Lévi-Strauss
Structuralism and Sociological Theory

C. R. Badcock

Holmes & Meier Publishers
New York

First published in the United States of America 1976 by
Holmes & Meier Publishers, Inc
101 Fifth Avenue
New York, New York 10003

© 1975 by C. R. Badcock

HM
24
B23
1976

Library of Congress Cataloging in Publication Data
Badcock, C. R.
    Lévi-Strauss: structuralism and sociological theory.

    Bibliography: p.
    Includes index.
    1. Sociology. 2. Lévi-Strauss, Claude. 3. Structuralism.
4. Social structure.
HM24.B23 1976   301'045   75–45308
ISBN 0–8419–0258–5

Printed in Great Britain

'Anthropology must be ecumenical.'
Salvador Dali
(Descharnes, *World of Dali*, p. 68)

Contents

Preface

This is not a book written by a believer in structuralism. If it were, I do not think that it would be very helpful to those to whom it is principally addressed. It is a book written for those whose interest in structuralism, and in Lévi-Strauss in particular, arises mainly from a concern with the place of structuralism and its major exponent in modern sociology and anthropology. I have written it very much from the point of view of sociological theory and the history of sociological thought. Students of the social sciences and the general reader who has some familiarity with the field will, I hope, find it useful. Those who know more about structuralism, and particularly about Lévi-Strauss, will probably not always agree with me, but will, I hope, find what I have to say worthy of consideration. Specialists will probably be scandalized by the absence of structuralist jargon and an approach which may appear too simple for the works of a writer such as Lévi-Strauss. For this I am unrepentant, and feel that, given the limited aims of this book, intelligibility takes priority over faithful adherence to the master's frequently untraceable footsteps through the labyrinth of structuralism.

As far as my own safe passage through it is concerned, I owe a debt of gratitude to Professors Donald MacRae, David Martin and Ernest Gellner, and especially to Professor Percy Cohen.

C.B.

1   Origins in Comte, Durkheim and Mauss

The aims of the book

The principal interest of Lévi-Strauss, both to students of the social sciences and to the reading public in general, is that he is the most well-known and widely read author belonging to what has now become known as the structuralist school. This is a label which he himself clearly accepts, using it a number of times in his works, and in the title of at least two of them. Certainly, as far as the social sciences are concerned, one might feel quite confident in calling Lévi-Strauss, the leader of the movement, or, at the very least, its most prominent exponent in the fields of anthropology and sociology.

The interest of structuralism as a movement in the social sciences originates from its claim, implicit or explicit as the case may be, to give a new insight, or consciousness, of man and his doings. This is something which is basic to all human sciences, and to sociology, anthropology and psychology in particular. Because man participates subjectively in being man, and because his works constitute his own subjective awareness, all of these sciences have striven from their very beginnings to give man a new insight into himself and a new consciousness of the society of which he is a part. The principal appeal of structuralism lies in the fact that it has attempted to do this in what appears to be a rather new way.

It has offered explanations of man and culture in terms of what Chomsky has called 'deep structures'. These 'deep structures' are principles of mental functioning which are unconscious but which structuralism attempts to uncover and, in anthropology and sociology at least, to reveal as the true basis of the phenomenon of culture. In attempting to uncover these collective and unconscious determinants of behaviour structuralism plays in the social sciences a rôle analogous to that of psychoanalysis in individual psychology.

Both claim to give a new awareness, a deeper insight into processes which affect us, but of which, until these disciplines emerged, we were largely unaware. And as we shall see later, it is one of the principal aims of this book to show just how much structuralism owes to psychoanalysis.

The desire to have a new consciousness of society, a new insight into culture is, in my opinion, the chief appeal of the social sciences in general, both to students entering on university courses in these disciplines, and to the general public in reading about them. The nature of the hoped-for new consciousness does, of course, vary widely. Some regard the study of sociology and social anthropology as a means of personal liberation from social forces which previously constrained them, but which, once understood for what they are, can be transcended by the individual. In this respect the social sciences play the part of the unmasker of mystifications, the debunker of myths, and the university becomes the slaughter-house for sacred cows. Others look to the social sciences for a consciousness of the realities which underlie the social structure which affects all of us and whose processes we all participate in. Since participation is to a large extent obligatory, it is as well if we can have some reliable information about exactly what we are a part of. Sociology and the study of contemporary social structures in particular is seen as a means to the end of a more rational awareness of social, political and economic realities, and, it is hoped, a more reliable basis for policy decisions.

Others again see the sciences of man and society as giving principally an insight into ourselves, as expanding our subjective awareness in such a way that, for instance, the unintelligible ritual of primitive peoples or even the irrational actions of members of our own society become comprehensible and a part of a meaningful picture of our own social experience.

To all of these interests structuralism appears to have something to offer and, as a new awareness of man and society, it appears to be worthy, at least initially, of our serious interest and a genuine attempt on our part to understand what it has to say.

Of course, it is not the first movement in the social sciences to hold out such a hope. Indeed, as I have already indicated, all social scientists have, in one way or another, offered something similar; all have claimed to give at least some sort of new insight into social reality, and it is my belief that if we really wish to understand structuralism and Lévi-Strauss, rather than merely learn to mouth its jargon and repeat at appropriate moments its clichés, then we must see structuralism and Lévi-Strauss' contribution to it against the background of the social sciences in general, and of the history of sociological theory in particular.

This, then, is the first aim of this book and the one to which I have devoted the first chapter. I want to try to show that the problems which the work of Lévi-Strauss can be seen to confront were bequeathed to him by an earlier generation of sociologists, and by Durkheim in particular. Furthermore, it is generally true that we can only reliably assess the significance of someone's contribution, in whatever field it may be, if we see it in the context of what went before it and what brought it into existence. No other book so far written on Lévi-Strauss has attempted to do this, and in doing it I have found it necessary, as the reader will soon see, to go back to the foundations of sociology in Comte and the Enlightenment. This is because the French sociological tradition to which Lévi-Strauss belongs begins with this and because, as we shall see in a moment, I believe that Lévi-Strauss' position in the history of sociology can only be accurately assessed against the background of its whole expanse.

My second main aim is to examine Lévi-Strauss from the *sociological* point of view. Plenty of books and articles have been published which look at his work from the standpoint of anthropology, linguistics, literary criticism or structuralism in general (the latter usually being the most unintelligible), but few, if any, have ever written about it in the way in which we are accustomed to finding Durkheim, Marx or Comte written about. The great weakness of previous studies in my opinion is that by treating Lévi-Strauss as *an* anthropologist, or *a* structuralist or as a structural linguistic bull in a socio-anthropological china-shop they have reduced the significance of his writings by ignoring their wide philosophical, sociological and methodological implications.

Consequently, my third most important aim will be to try to penetrate to this level of general sociological and methodological interest in Lévi-Strauss' work and to reveal, for what I believe will be the first time, the fundamental philosophical and methodological groundwork of his structuralism. I shall try to show that, as a sociologist and theoretician, Lévi-Strauss can be profitably compared with other sociologists on the same sort of basis which, for instance, one might compare Comte with Pareto. Indeed, more than this, I intend to show that precisely the same theoretical and methodological issues which sociologists are habituated to finding and discussing in the works of such classical writers can also be found in Lévi-Strauss' structuralism. This will lead us eventually to a consideration of what is probably the most important of these issues both from the point of view of understanding what Lévi-Strauss is saying and from that of realizing what may be wrong in his approach. This is his reductionism. Most people who read his works soon gather that he is in some way or another reducing some aspects of culture to the operation of the mind. But few realize just how he goes about doing this, and still less how notions like Nature as a final reductive explanation enter into his system. Few other writers have directed much attention to this, but it will be my aim to reveal just what Lévi-Strauss' reductionism reduces to and to demonstrate that it is in fact far less incomprehensible, metaphysical and original than many appear to suspect. Finally, I shall attempt to show that Lévi-Strauss' structuralism is in fact just a new version of psychoanalysis, but one which, like all psychoanalytic heresies, denies the body and in this case dresses up the ideas of Freud in the trappings of cybernetics.

Sociology as a religion

New intellectual movements like structuralism do not, of course, originate out of nothing. As an intellectual phenomenon virgin birth is unknown. Paternity always exists, even if it is frequently doubtful. My aim in this book is to demonstrate just what the paternity of Lévi-Strauss' structuralism is, and to show that, far from being new and unfamiliar, it does in fact go back to problems in sociological theory and anthropological practice which existed at the very emergence of these disciplines and which have continued to affect their course ever since. As I have remarked, I intend to try to show that Lévi-Strauss' version of structuralism, probably the most complete and coherently thought-out that we have in the social sciences, is firmly grounded in traditional sociological and anthropological thought, and that its new and interesting pronouncements can be seen to be attempting solutions to some old and very intractable problems.

Logically enough, the most important of Lévi-Strauss' contributions to sociological thought go back to the most fundamental problems that sociology encounters, and I shall attempt to show how Lévi-Strauss, in the course of his works, has attempted to resolve them. We shall see, I hope, that not only is this an excellent way of realizing how this new and apparently unfamiliar type of analysis relates to the great traditions and continuities of sociological thought, but that also it provides the best and most reliable means of understanding just what it is that Lévi-Strauss is saying, given that his mode of expression is not always exactly easy to understand. We shall find that a systematic progress through these fundamental problems and Lévi-Strauss' answers to them is also a clear guide through his works, and we shall also perhaps not be surprised, knowing what we do of the Gallic flair for logic, to find that a logical progression from the most fundamental to the most recondite and rarefied of these sociological questions also entails a more or less strictly chronological consideration of his works.

But if we wish to begin at the beginning of Lévi-Strauss, both logically and chronologically, then we must, as I have suggested, also begin at the beginning of sociology. The reason for this is that Lévi-Strauss' first major work, his *Structures élémentaires de la parenté* (translated into English as *Elementary Structures of Kinship*), while ostensibly being a weighty anthropological study of kinship systems, can in fact be seen to be an attempt at solving one of the most intractable problems of sociological theory, a problem which Lévi-Strauss inherited from Durkheim, his most important predecessor in French sociology, but one which is still very much a theoretical difficulty today and which can be found in the works of many other writers. In order to understand just what this problem is, and consequently to be in a position to appreciate the significance of Lévi-Strauss' resolution of it, we must first trace it back to Durkheim's major predecessor, Comte, the first of the modern sociologists and the founding father with whom this difficulty really began. The difficulty in question is not merely widespread, but, as I must now attempt to show, of fundamental importance to sociology as a whole; and like most of its really significant methodological problems, one which springs from one of its most important strengths. In attempting to resolve it, albeit implicitly rather than explicitly, Lévi-Strauss was himself to be the equal of Comte and Durkheim in exploring the most fundamental issues of sociological theory, and his contributions to the problem make him worthy of as much close theoretical scrutiny as has been given to his two great forerunners in French sociology. Lévi-Strauss may have presented himself to the public principally as an anthropologist, but, like others before him such as Radcliffe-Brown and Malinowski, he is an anthropologist whose work is rich in sociological insights and whose position on the major theoretical issues of sociology other sociologists cannot afford to ignore.

In assessing Lévi-Strauss' significance for sociology as a whole and his contribution to its persisting theoretical and methodological difficulties it is therefore a good idea to look back for a moment over the history of sociological thought and to try to see just how he fits into it.

The first period of sociological thought, running roughly from the beginning of the nineteenth century to the end of its third quarter, was what one might term the Age of the Prophets. It was dominated by prophetic figures like St Simon, Comte and Marx.

Each one of these was a lonely exception in the intellectual life of his times. Each lived a more or less precarious existence, deriving little or nothing in the way of material or any other kind of profit from his works. Each expostulated on the present and future state of society in a highly rhetorical and frequently apocalyptic vein. Marx, with his patriarchal head, Jewish looks and unkempt appearance, comes closest to the Old Testament prototype; but Comte and St Simon might equally be seen as prophets of a new science and a new social order. Indeed, the churches which these two founded appear to qualify them for the title of 'Prophet of Sociology' with great justice.

The next epoch was dominated by the 'classical' sociologists, especially Durkheim and Weber, but also including Tönnies, Simmel and Pareto. The prophets had written visionary books, often concerned with great issues and above all with the future, whether it was the positive or communist revelation as the case may be. The great classical sociologists produced the most famous sociological studies of specific things – one recalls in this context Durkheim's

Suicide and *Elementary Forms of the Religious Life*, Weber's *Protestant Ethic and the Spirit of Capitalism, Religion of China*, and some of the classic studies of Tönnies and Simmel. These sociologists were the first to become accepted into the intellectual and political life of their epochs. No one exemplifies the new respectability of sociology and sociologists in this period better than Durkheim, who occupied the first chair of sociology to be created in any university. Weber, too, had a university chair, and all of these sociologists were in one sense or another accepted into society, rather than remaining lonely figures protesting without it, as had been the lot of Comte, St Simon and Marx.

Towards the end of this period – following the First World War – a new tendency became visible in sociology, particularly in the later works of Weber and Pareto. This was a tendency to turn away from specific, classic studies to general theorizing. This involved both Pareto and Weber in constructing typologies of 'social action', an attempt to ground sociological theory in an explanatory framework covering all forms of human behaviour seen in a social context. In the third and most recent period of sociological thought this tendency to general theorizing came to fruition, particularly in the great works of Talcott Parsons – his *Structure of Social Action* and *The Social System*. Here the concern with the classification of types of social action reaches its highest point, and so too does the desire to develop an all-embracing system of sociological theory. Another, and, in the case of Lévi-Strauss, most important aspect of the contemporary sociological approach, is an attempt to resolve contradictions within sociology itself, and in particular to reconcile conflicting theoretical viewpoints derived from the great prophets and classical founding fathers.

In this respect the history of sociology is remarkably like that of many religions. Typically, the religion begins with a single prophetic founder. This is the original 'Voice crying in the Wilderness'. Such voices make little impression in their own day, but later a group of dedicated followers forms itself, and the followers of isolated prophets become a sect. Very rapidly, ideological leaders emerge whose job it is to lay down the true, authentic teaching of the master, to define heresy and erroneous interpretations of his words, and to combat schismatic tendencies.

In the history of Christianity, St Paul is the most obvious example of this. In terms of my analogy, the Apostle to the Gentiles would correspond to Weber (that is, if we interpret *The Protestant Ethic* and other works as an attempt to resolve contradictions in Marx's theory of social change and to bring out neglected aspects of the situation). In the course of this epoch, the sect becomes a church and the prophet's message becomes religious dogma. In time, the third and last phase supervenes, that of *Scholasticism*.

As the message of the master becomes widely accepted and orthodox dogma well defined, a tendency towards the elaboration of finer points of doctrine emerges which goes along with a drift towards greater acceptance of the existing social and political *status quo*. The new religion, its childhood and adolescence now over, enters on maturity. In organizational terms this means the church becoming legitimated and being integrated into the wider society – corresponding to the acceptance of sociology within the university in my analogy. But in theological and philosophical terms it means an effort to accommodate and reconcile traditional ideas and, more importantly, to develop a formulation of the doctrine which can be easily taught to students. In Christianity this tendency begins with St Augustine and reaches its culmination in St Thomas Aquinas, who in terms of my metaphor corresponds to Talcott Parsons. By the time we have reached the Scholastic epoch, the doctrine is being presented in huge textbooks, clearly set out, as in *The Structure of Social Action* and St Thomas's *Summa Theologiae*, with pedagogic considerations uppermost in mind. The logical consistency and inclusiveness of the system is stressed and all previous thought is made to appear to move towards this final, and definitive summation. Hence Aristotle is made to appear a good Catholic and reconciled with the Pseudo-Dionysius (by all accounts a Neo-Platonist) by St Thomas, and Marx is made to fit himself in with Durkheim, Marshall, Pareto *et al.* by Parsons. The theoretician in this period is motivated to give complete, all-embracing and final answers to all questions, to leave no ends untied, and to unify all knowledge, all conflicting tendencies, into one single work which is both a compendium and a synthesis of all previous writings on the subject.

Lévi-Strauss clearly does not belong among the prophets, but neither does he among the classical writers. His place must be, if my analogy has any validity at all, among the scholastics. He has not, it is true, produced such obviously scholastic works as Talcott Parsons has done, but it is my aim to show that essentially Lévi-Strauss' theoretical approach to sociology is synthetic, that it draws on the classical writers and attempts to reconcile them and that it aims to give exhaustive answers on the subjects which it considers. Certainly from the literary point of view his works bear all the marks of the scholastic mind. They are long-winded, jargon-ridden, highly technical, frequently obscure and always extremely erudite and full of references, both overt and hidden, to the classical writers such as Durkheim, Marx and to other sources as well.

If we are expecting Lévi-Strauss to exhibit sociological theories and methodological approaches which are quite new and unfamiliar we shall be greatly disappointed. In fact, it will be my aim to show that theoretically speaking, he belongs to his generation, is highly comparable to Talcott Parsons, and scholastic in flavour. We shall see that he draws very heavily on Durkheim, Marx and Freud in particular, and that the structural linguistics to be found in his works which is made so much of by other writers is almost of minor significance and functions mainly to provide theoretical and logical props on which to hang remnants of the classical theories. We shall see that his Marxism only makes sense if we see it as highly Durkheimianized, and his Durkheimian positivism only if blended with something from Marx. All the rest is Freud.

But before we begin to draw our conclusions let us first make a beginning, and in particular let us see just to what extent my comparison of sociology with religion holds water. If we begin by looking at Comte, the founder of sociology, we shall begin to understand much of what Durkheim, and later Lévi-Strauss, were to try to do.

Earlier on I spoke about the aspirations of sociology with regard to giving its students a new insight into things – a new social consciousness. The first of the great theoretical issues which I want to look at in connection with Lévi-Strauss' works and which derives from Durkheim can in fact be detected in Comte's attempt to provide exactly this – a new consciousness of social reality. This new consciousness Comte called positivism, and it is clearly defined in the famous 'Law of the Three Stages'. Comte enunciates this law as follows:

. . . each branch of our knowledge passes successively through three different theoretical conditions, the Theological, or fictitious, the Metaphysical, or abstract, and the Scientific, or positive. In other words, the human mind, by its nature employs in its progress three methods of philosophising, the character of each one of which is essentially different, even radically opposed. . . . The first is the necessary point of departure for the human understanding, the third is fixed and definite state. The second is merely a state of transition.[1]

This new consciousness is the scientific consciousness. In the first stage, the Theological, absolute knowledge is sought by reference to the acts of spiritual beings. In the second these become rationalized into an abstract idea such as God, or Nature. But Comte's positive philosophy seeks to reduce all phenomena to 'aspects of a single general fact – such as gravitation, for instance'.[2] But the positive knowledge thus obtained would not be purely theoretical. Comte too hoped that sociological science would have practical uses. 'The positive philosophy', he says, 'offers the only solid basis for the social reorganization which must succeed the critical conditions in which the most civilized nations are now living'.[3]

But not all departments of knowledge would reach this positive stage at the same time. 'Knowledge', says Comte, 'reaches the positive stage early in proportion to its generality, simplicity and independence of other departments.'[4] It comes as no surprise to learn that he sees mathematics as historically the first of the positive sciences, followed by astronomy, 'terrestrial physics', chemistry and biology – the latter two only reaching the positive stage in Comte's own day. Finally, what Comte at first called 'social physics', but later christened, by a solecism, 'sociology', would become a positive science as well. And what is more, this new science, sociology, was to be supreme in the Hierarchy of Sciences. What theology had once been – the Queen of the Sciences – sociology was now to become. For the hierarchy was not one merely of historical evolution, listing the order in which branches of knowledge had dispelled their primeval theologico-metaphysical gloom, it was also and perhaps more importantly a logical hierarchy. Each science depended on the one beneath it, so that astronomy, for example, depended on a positive mathematics in order to be positive itself. But, also, each science was independent. Biology, for instance, could not be entirely reduced to chemistry in Comte's view. A certain irreducible residuum remained in each which meant that, within its own sphere of competence, each science could handle its own explanations without recourse necessarily to that immediately below it in the hierarchy.

This sounds perfectly reasonable in the context of chemistry or biology, but in that of sociology it hides a difficulty which we shall find recurring in Durkheim and to which Lévi-Strauss addresses himself while attempting to resolve the complexities of primitive kinship systems. The special difficulty here with regard to sociology is that this science is seen as paramount in the hierarchy and consequently one which could not be the basis for anything else. Each field of knowledge in Comte's hierarchy was both itself more complex than that which went before it and, naturally enough, competent to study a reality more complicated than those lower down. If sociology were the Queen of the Sciences, then it follows that sociology would address itself to the most complex reality known to man, to the highest order of things that existed, namely Society itself. In this respect there was a close analogy with the now superseded science of theology, and this went even further when we recall that since each science in the hierarchy cannot wholly be reduced to a subordinate one but must explain its own reality in its own irreducible terms, then sociology – the study of the highest and most complex reality – had to explain that reality, in part at least, in terms which could not be reduced to anything else. In other words, society, to some extent, was self-explanatory. Now it is easy to see that this is another respect in which sociology comes to resemble theology, for theology too in its heyday presumed to study the highest and most transcendant reality – God – who was defined in metaphysical terms as a self-subsistent being, or, to put it another way, as a self-explanatory reality. It is easy to see the temptation to regard society as a replacement for God in at least some sort of sense approximating to the meaning of the term in theology. And, indeed, as we shall see, Comte did succumb completely to this temptation to equate society with God, and sociology with theology, while Durkheim, as I hope to show, succumbed to the extent that he retained moral and metaphysical vestiges of the idea.

Put in contemporary sociological jargon, this is the problem of holism – of seeing society as greater than the sum of its parts, and as transcending individuals. But it is also more than this, and, as we shall see, is in fact the root of a number of fundamental difficulties in sociological explanation, even in the structuralist explanations of Lévi-Strauss.

For the moment, let us conclude that Comte invented the idea of a new positive and scientific consciousness of social reality – an idea to which all subsequent and contemporary sociologists are committed in one way or another, Lévi-Strauss included – and that having created this new branch of knowledge, went on to turn it, in accordance with the principle that all revolutionaries restore the worst elements of the abuses which they most want to eradicate, into a more or less exact replica of what it was meant to replace – namely, theology. It comes then as no surprise to see Comte, under the influence of his passion for a young Parisienne named Clothilde Vaux, founding a positive church and at the end of his life writing to the head of the Society of Jesus in an attempt to convert the Jesuits to the new religion and signing himself 'Founder of the Universal Religion, High Priest of Humanity'. Sociologists usually pass over Comte's Positive Religion in silence, or dismiss it as the aberrant fantasy of an ageing *savant* under the influence of a hysterical young woman. But as I have attempted to suggest, its origins lie in the very essence of Comte's sociology itself, and it is undeniable that the Positive Religion follows on logically from the Law of the Three Stages, the Hierarchy of the Sciences, and a belief in the importance of religious institutions for man and society. Later sociologists, like Durkheim, were to be greatly embarrassed by Comte's positivistic excesses, but here, as is so often the case, pathology teaches an important lesson about normality, and the reappearance of the trappings of religion in Comte is of profound significance for our understanding of the theoretical basis of sociology.

Durkheim

In Durkheim the problem reappears in a different form, but we shall encounter it just as surely when we come to consider the final formulations of Durkheim's theoretical position and its relation to Lévi-Strauss' analysis of totemism. For the time being, let us recall that Durkheim, in his *Rules of Sociological Method*, resolutely sets out to rid sociology of the worst excesses of Comte's positive philosophy. A number of times he repeats his desire to reject 'mere ideas', and instead to base a science of society on a solid foundation of empirical fact. As I shall now try to show, it was this attempt to talk only in terms of social facts that led Durkheim, in his turn, into theoretical difficulties and methodological contradictions exactly analogous to those which led Comte to the Positive Religion, and to whose resolution Lévi-Strauss was to offer the analysis of society which we find in *Elementary Structures of Kinship* and *The Savage Mind*.

Durkheim's task, as he saw it, was to put sociology on a firmer empirical basis. Like Comte he believed that the study of society should become scientific, and if this is what we call positivism then he believed in it as much as Comte had done. But Durkheim meant by positivism something very different from what Comte had meant. To begin with, Durkheim did not mean a philosophy of life, a religion. Unlike Comte, who began with the enlightened (Enlightenment) moral principles and humanist inspiration and then proceeded to found a science of sociology to justify and to complete it:

Founding Universal Religion upon the True Philosophy which has been extracted from Real Science[5]

Durkheim began with a scientific sociology and hoped, perhaps a little naïvely, that it would lead in the end to some ethical conclusions.[6] Durkheim represents a development in the positive tradition. Comte was close enough to the Enlightenment for his faith in Reason (Reason with the capital 'R', Voltaire's Reason, Robespierre's 'Cult of Reason') to be strong enough to justify the higher flights of the Positive Philosophy.

Durkheim, living in the troubled epoch of the Dreyfus Affair, the Boulanger Débâcle and the anarchist bombings, found his faith in the goddess of Reason somewhat shaken. In fact, he had little faith in it at all, otherwise he would have been a philosopher like Comte. But Durkheim did not wish to imitate Comte in this. Positivism had retreated from philosophy and in Durkheim's system positivism became identified exclusively with the methods of the empirical sciences. Yet the desire for a 'social science', for a science which would teach the ways and means of social reconstruction, of sociological understanding, still existed. Durkheim did not wholly despair of positivism, he merely clipped its wings, and in doing so brought it down from high flights of mystical fervour to the solid ground of empirical research.

For Durkheim, then, social science in the true sense, in Comte's sense, 'Sociology' in fact, was not an impossible positivist dream, but rather a perfectly viable endeavour which had been started on, but spoilt by too much pretension and by unrealistic expectations. Given this, Durkheim's procedure seemed clear. It consisted first of all in going back to the origins of sociology[7] – to the figures who stood behind Comte, who had begun what Comte had spoilt by his exaggerations – and then in proceeding to develop a new sociology, an empirical, comparative sociology free from 'mere ideas'.[8]

At first sight, this might appear a rather difficult undertaking since everything the social scientist studies is embodied in ideas – the family is an idea, society is an idea, even suicide is an idea – and all these ideas involve problems of definition, and are open to purely philosophical, even to metaphysical controversy. Durkheim's solution was to maintain quite dogmatically (and when we recall Comte his dogmatism is understandable) that we should treat social facts *'comme les choses'*. These social facts that were going to be treated as things were, Durkheim argued, 'things' in a real sense. Philosophically speaking, a 'thing', in the sense which Durkheim intends it, is something which is outside our immediate subjectivity, it is something which has an independent existence. When Durkheim talked of treating social facts as 'things' he meant by this that they should be ascribed a certain independent ontological status, he meant them to have actuality independent of our consciousness. Hence a dream as experienced by a dreamer is not a thing in this sense – it is an element of subjective experience – but dreams may be treated as things if we regard them as phenomena independent of our immediate volition and subjective interest. As such, we must hold in abeyance our personal opinion of dreams and look at them instead in objective terms, which is as much to say that we must regard them in empirical, measurable, scientific terms. Let us take suicide as an instance. Clearly, we can all adopt a subjective attitude to suicide. We can all say whether we agree with it, deplore it, applaud it, or whatever. We can each of us try to find out what suicide is by attempting it, or by trying to imagine what it is like. But, equally, we can adopt an objective viewpoint, holding our personal opinions in abeyance and studying suicide as a 'thing', just as we might study the weather or a chemical substance. For Durkheim, physical science only enjoys a certain priority here because it has never been encumbered with 'mere ideas' – or at least, if once it was then they have been easily shed. It makes no sense to have an opinion about the moral rights and wrongs of the periodic table of elements, or the English weather. These are facts, undebatable, controvertible in terms of scientific theory, but unknowable in terms of personal subjectivity. No one knows how it 'feels' to be a chemical element. Durkheim's point is that people have concentrated too much on what makes people 'feel' like committing suicide.

It follows from all this that the social fact can be defined as something independent of individuals' volition and immediate intention. A person's remarks about an event do not immediately constitute a social fact since what the person says may be totally false and lacking any basis in reality. But a sequence of events, viewed as a sequence of events, as being something bigger than the scope of the individual's immediate action – a strike for instance, or accident statistics – can quite easily be treated as a social fact. Thus whereas a suicide constitutes a social fact in this sense, a person's conscious reasons for committing suicide do not of necessity do so. They have a certain basis in social fact as Durkheim laboured to show in his *Suicide*, but we cannot take the conscious expression at its face value as a 'fact'. A sufficiently objective criterion however can be provided by either a statistical summation of events (as in *Suicide*), or by structural summation of phenomena. For example, a single gesture made by a single person is not a social fact *prima facie* – it is a personal one, but not necessarily a social one. If, however, it is repeated by a large number of people we are justified in saying that the gesture, shall we say genuflection in churches, is not an individual eccentricity but a social, structural regularity – a norm.

Empirical, positive sociology for Durkheim comes down to being the study of norms, statistical on the one hand, structural on the other. His two major works, *Suicide* and *Elementary Forms of the Religious Life*, are examples of the former and the latter.

This realization, of what we might term in modern jargon the 'normative' basis of social studies, leads Durkheim to conceive of the social fact as being the outcome of something coercive with regard to the individual, and the individual came to be seen as a mere actor, or, in more recent terms, a 'rôle player', as a deviating, chaotic singularity only given place and significance in the system by structural norms.

Durkheim, in a work written with the collaboration of Mauss, characterized this sociological method by the well-chosen name 'Sociocentrics'.[9] It should now be obvious why. Since for Durkheim social regularities – norms – are to be seen as the basis of social order, and since sociology can only explain by reference to these, then it is clear that all explanation will be in terms of the whole society rather than in terms of individual action. A consideration of Durkheim's 'Sociology of Knowledge' will elucidate this point.

The reasons for resorting to the 'Sociocentric' theory of knowledge can be seen as follows. Durkheim needs to explain the origin of ideas. He cannot have recourse to God, or to something like Transcendental Idealism. The only solution is to be found in Sociocentrism. Put very simply, Durkheim's theory set out in *Elementary Forms* and elsewhere is that all ideas and categories of thought have a social origin. They originate in the *conscience collective*, and all social facts come to be seen as representations of this collective consciousness, as *représentations collectives*. This is as true of ideas, even philosophical ones, as it is of table manners, or crime statistics – indeed, in the *Rules* Durkheim ingeniously shows how crime, a deviation from the *conscience collective*, is entirely normal and therefore no real deviation at all. I think that the term 'sociocentric' will be seen to be entirely apt in describing this theory.

But this emphasis on the central and independent rôle of society, whilst bringing about the autonomy of the science of sociology, also involved it in a number of insoluble difficulties. These problems are clearly highlighted in a remark made by Durkheim and Mauss in their *Primitive Classification*. At the very end of this work, Durkheim and Mauss state that these representations, in this case those of primitive systems of classification, are not logically ordered, but find their principles of relationship in the emotional and the collective. Indeed, in the penultimate paragraph they tell us:

. . . emotion is naturally refractory to analysis, or at least, lends itself uneasily to it, because it is too complex. Above all, when it has a collective origin it defies critical and rational examination.[10]

On this note they end their book.

A moment's reflection will suffice to show that this is an extraordinary admission for a so-called positivist to make. It is, quite simply, an admission of defeat. Durkheim has succeeded in establishing the basis of a science; with admirable lucidity he has laid down the rules for the isolation of its subject matter, principles for the definition of normal and pathological states, a basis for the classification of social types, and so on. But at the point of explaining the necessity of the relationships between the representations Durkheim's system fails us. Failing to find a rational necessity in the relationships of these classifications, he resorts to what can only be a solution of despair and declares them to be possessed of an emotional necessity, presumed inexplicable, or at least, explicable only in terms of irrational and irreducible qualities.

In other words, the states of collective activity which give rise to the fundamental representations on which systems of social classification like totemism are based are presumed by Durkheim to be totally inexplicable. What is more, this negative and unpositivistic conclusion suggests that the *conscience collective* is an ultimately irreducible and inexplicable reality which, as we have already seen, is the final term in Durkheim's explanatory system. Durkheim traces everything to the *conscience collective* declaring that 'The first logical categories are social categories' but the social categories – which derive from the *conscience collective* – defy 'critical and rational examination'. His theory may be sociocentric but what it centres on appears to be a sociological 'Cloud of Unknowing'. This is a slight and almost wholly methodological vestige of Comte's quasi-theological approach to sociology, but one which will be of some significance to us in our attempt to understand the importance of Lévi-Strauss' contributions to sociological theory. Essentially, it is a failure on Durkheim's part to provide a genuinely *reductive* explanation of social phenomena. Another way of saying the same thing is to remark that it is also a failure to provide an explanation of the causal connection between the social whole – *the conscience collective* – and the individual. We see in terms of sociocentric explanation how the collectivity affects the individual (through education, rituals, social control etc), but we do not see how the individual contributes to the social whole, except, that is, in terms of inexplicable states of collective emotion. Finally one might point out that for Durkheim the *conscience collective* played the rôle of God in the sphere of moral and ethical activity in a most unmistakable way. According to him, only society was powerful enough and important enough to lay down the moral code for its members. In the moral sense, society, like God, was omnipotent, omniscient and omnipresent.

To sum up, then, Durkheim, while eradicating the worst effects of Comte's positivism, nevertheless retained society – or, more strictly, the *conscience collective* – as a quasi-metaphysical, and certainly a moral entity, transcending individuals and, in certain respects, inscrutable to science. For Durkheim, positivism had not created a religion of humanity but had caused him to see human societies as possessing quasi-divine attributes, and in particular as being the source of all moral values, philosophical ideas and social norms. Apart from this, Durkheim was incapable of accounting for the origin of these collective representations, or social facts, and it is to Lévi-Strauss' resolution of this problem that we shall turn in the next chapter.

Mauss

But before we go on, it is necessary to look briefly at one other sociologist of the French tradition who has had a great deal of influence over Lévi-Strauss' thinking and one who provides the link between the subject of our study and Durkheim. This person is Marcel Mauss, Durkheim's co-author in *Primitive Classification*. It is perhaps ironic that I should have picked on a quotation from this book to exemplify the most serious shortcomings of Durkheim's sociological analysis because I am now going to present Durkheim's collaborator as a sociologist who in his own independent works went some considerable way to resolving the problems left over by Durkheim and provided Lévi-Strauss with one of the principal means by which the latter was to transcend the limitations of the Durkheimian system. Mauss did this in what is probably his most widely read work, *L'Essai sur le don*, known to us as *The Gift*.

The significance of this quite exemplary sociological treatise is that it is at the same time a successful application, and an important development of Durkheim's method of sociological analysis.

Seen from the surface, and without enquiring into its implicit methodology, *The Gift* is a perfect example of the orthodox Durkheimian procedure. Mauss isolates a group of sociological facts – various forms of gift-giving in various societies – justifies the 'factuality' of the institution by pointing out its obligatory nature, and ends by formulating a set of sociological laws which can be seen to determine and to explain gift-giving and receiving in all its various and complex forms.

However, if we look deeper, we see that in fact Mauss, although faithful to all of Durkheim's methodological rules, has gone somewhat further than his master in his analysis, and has been led to the realization of a new principle which, when developed as it was to be in the work of Lévi-Strauss, was to enable sociology to transcend the narrow confines of Durkheim's rather closed functionalism and to expand into new, fertile fields of investigation. This realization was Mauss' isolation of the principle of reciprocity.

As I shall try to show later, the principle of reciprocity and its implications are an important foundation of the structuralist approach in sociology. Mauss' main significance for structural social studies, and for Lévi-Strauss in particular, is the way in which, whilst giving a functional explanation in its most lucid form, he also incorporated a deeper methodological insight, an insight which was eventually to lead sociology not only to describe particular institutions in functional terms, but to explain why the particular form of the institution existed.

At first sight, there is nothing particularly new or very original in Mauss' analysis. One can easily imagine how a doctrinaire functionalist might assimilate the idea. Reciprocity is shown by Mauss to be an essential 'norm' in the societies studied, a norm which, on account of the high functional integration of those societies, resulted in gift-giving assuming a 'total' social significance, a significance for which a rule of reciprocity was essential.

But this approach will not translate Mauss' analysis without residue into functionalist terms, for there is more than this in what he is saying. In any case, such a formulation would not do. Certainly, gifts are given and reciprocated because there is a norm in society that they should be. But to speak solely in such terms gives the impression that in primitive societies – or in modern ones, for that matter – all is harmony and concord. Unless the idea of a normative consensus is reduced to a sociological cliché of questionable validity, any stronger interpretation will inevitably either lead back to Durkheimian metaphysics, or to a naïve assumption of universal harmony in society.

What essentially Mauss achieves in *The Gift* is not to give us a superior functional analysis which will get over these frequently encountered difficulties, rather, he gives us a totally new perspective on this institution of gift-giving, one that happily coexists with an intelligent functionalism but transcends it entirely in its implications and explanatory power. The essence of this approach is that it looks at social phenomena not in terms of their relation to a society's subjectivity – its norms – nor to its content – its system of values – but rather it analyses phenomena in terms of their form and on the basis of an objectivity.

In the case of *The Gift*, Mauss achieves this in part at least by giving great weight to the need for reciprocity and by seeing this reciprocity not only in its normative, but also in its structural implications, for a norm of reciprocity will ensure that a system of communication can function where gifts are concerned. Hence, in the case of Trobriand *Kula*, for instance, islanders belonging to different societies, with differing *consciences collectives* (as different as those of Dobu and the Trobriands) can maintain a system that ensures wide inter-island communication, and which can be shown to work not on account of the norms which govern it considered simply as norms, but rather on account of the implicit structure of the system as a set of logical relations, an implicit structure whose own inner logical necessity determines the norms, rather than conversely. Seen as a logical game, as a system of communication, this analysis of gift-giving easily coexists with the Durkheimian view. But it is interesting to note that while Mauss, like Durkheim, thinks a moral conclusion to be right for sociological investigation, he draws a moral conclusion of quite a different sort. Whereas Durkheim talks vaguely of a new occupational basis for this collective consciousness,[11] Mauss talks instead[12] of a structural solution, of a solution to modern problems of want and injustice quite independent of attitudes. Hence he recommends systems of workers' insurance etc, systems which will, because of this systematic character, redistribute wealth in such a way that those processes of inner communication which underlie all social wholes will function on the basis of a new, and more thorough-going principle of reciprocity. For Mauss sees a principle of reciprocity guaranteeing equality for structural reasons, whereas Durkheim would see reciprocity as guaranteeing the social structure for moral reasons.

A concept of exchange immediately transforms the Sociocentric method. The limitations of this method were that it created a hiatus between the individual and the collective, that it seemed to explain only a one-way process of causation, and as such, failed to deal with the problem of social change. Mauss' systematics of exchange, however, completely alters this situation. Grafted on to Durkheim's Sociocentrics it allows us to retain what is valuable in the latter's formulations, but to reject his static functionalism, and to make up for the absence of a sociological dynamics.

The structural principle of reciprocity of necessity determines that a logically ordered system of exchanges should operate in a society, since the norm of reciprocity sets up a system of equivalences which must be respected. The exchanges, because reciprocal, reduce all to a common level, that of exchangers. Here the problem of the relation between the individual and society is solved. Individualism in the sociological sense does not enter into Durkheim's sociology, it is holistic. It does enter into Mauss' sociology because he succeeds where Durkheim failed, he succeeds in linking the individual with the whole, the one with the many.

In the system of gift exchange, all gift-givers exist as independent and individual actors, each of whom constitutes a creator of the system. His contribution to the system is directly mediated, as Mauss so clearly shows us, by the norm of reciprocity – so far thoroughly Durkheimian. But what Mauss' formulation allows, and what Durkheim's does not, is an explanation in reversed terms. The norm of reciprocity interpreted in a Durkheimian sense explains little, it leaves the question of causation open, since we are unenlightened as to the origin of the norm. Mauss merely invokes the norm as a description, and instead shows us that exchange, which is a reversible and two-way process, is necessitated by the requirement of reciprocity, and that reciprocity is necessitated by the requirement of exchange.

It may be objected that the formulation which I have just offered is no more enlightening than the Durkheimian one. In saying that Mauss held that exchange exists because of reciprocity and reciprocity because of exchange I appear to have said little that is more than the Durkheimian circularity of norm and society, and society and norm. But this is not the case; a consideration of the further implications of what I have just said will show why this is so.

Mauss, unlike Durkheim, has made a claim to a fundamental principle of sociological explanation. Where Durkheim's explanation of society is only in terms of the society itself, a Sociocentric theory – a theory which explains that society is social because it is social – Mauss gives us a theory which says in essence that society is what it is because there is communication. Mauss' actual proposition with regard to the gift is that the gift is what it is, an instrument of the collective, because it is a means of exchange, and an exchange of means. It only requires the addition of the basic concept of what the means is, namely a language, an arbitrary system of structurally determined differences, to provide us with what is in the truest sense a rounded theory of society. It is the synthesis of this theory by Lévi-Strauss in his *Elementary Structures of Kinship* which we will now go on to consider.

2   Culture as a language

Having looked briefly at some of the most important forerunners of Lévi-Strauss in French sociology, I now want to attempt to look at Lévi-Strauss' three most important works. These are *The Elementary Structures of Kinship, The Savage Mind* and *Mythologiques* (or, *A Science of Myth*). As I do so I shall bear in mind what was said in the first chapter about the methodological problems bequeathed to Lévi-Strauss by Durkheim and try to show how each one of these books contains, in part at least, a solution.

The problem, which in modern sociological jargon is that of holistic functionalism, in fact breaks down into three subsidiary problems. First, there is the question of the historical origin of social facts, and of the most important social fact, what Lévi-Strauss would call 'culture', and Durkheim would have called the *conscience collective*. Secondly, there is the problem of the structural, or logical origin of social facts, or the individualism versus holism controversy as it is often known. Finally, there is the question of social change and its accommodation within Durkheimism or functionalist systems of explanation (that is, systems of explanation which stress consensus and social wholes). The last of these questions will be dealt with in the next chapter, where I shall consider Lévi-Strauss' debt to Marxism. The first two – the question of the historical origins of social facts, we shall find Lévi-Strauss dealing with in his *Totemism, The Savage Mind* and *Elementary Structures of Kinship*.

Kinship

Although not generally applied by Mauss, the attitude towards society which I have attributed to him and which is based on considering society as a system of exchanges could obviously be

B

generalized as a sociological theory. It was precisely this which Lévi-Strauss attempted in his *Elementary Structures of Kinship* and it should come as no surprise to find him in the opening chapter of that book discussing Mauss' *The Gift* and the sociological principles it introduces. Inevitably, the more general application of these principles predicated not only a reductive explanation – a form of explanation which could reduce social phenomena to permutations of exchange – but also a historical reduction, a theory about the evolution of society through history, and more particularly a theory of the evolution of human societies from non-human, animal pre-history. For the great shortcomings of the Durkheimian explanation do not only manifest themselves as the lack of a truly reductive explanation in the present, they also do so with regard to the past. Durkheim, by reducing social phenomena to a collectivity, the *conscience collective*, effectively negated the reductive aspect of his explanation and ran into all the methodological difficulties which I have by now fully spelt out. What was lacking, as we have seen, was an explanation of the collective consciousness itself and the way in which individual consciousness constituted it, as well as an explanation of the representations – the structures of collective thought which composed it. This lack of explanations affected not only society in the present, but also how it had constituted itself in the past. Durkheim's sociocentrics involved logical problems in the synchronic aspects, but in relation to the past it represented a complete lack of any theory. Social facts, as Durkheim tells us in *The Rules*, should be explained by reference to antecedent social facts. If the collective consciousness, or society itself is taken as the supreme social fact then it is clear that there should be some antecedent social fact if explanation of it should be at all possible. As we shall now see, Lévi-Strauss in the opening chapters of *Elementary Structures of Kinship* is in fact postulating just such pre-social social fact.

At first sight such a thing might appear an impossibility. Nothing that is genuinely social could precede the appearance of society in a historical sense without involving us in a redefinition of 'social' which would in some way or another derive it without contradiction from 'natural'. Such an undertaking would certainly have appeared difficult, or absolutely impossible to Durkheim. For him it would have compromised the meaning of the word 'social'. We have only to recall his definition of what constituted the social fact and the related issues discussed in chapter 1 to see that this would be so. For Durkheim, as I tried to suggest in that chapter, what was peculiar to the social was its irreducibility to the personal, or the natural. We have already seen that Mauss did implicitly reduce the social to the personal and individual in a certain sense, and now we must go on to see how Lévi-Strauss contrives to do the same with regard to the 'natural' state which it is necessary to postulate before the appearance of the 'social' in the historical sense.

The requirements of the pre-social social fact, however paradoxical they may appear, might be met if a 'natural' social fact could be produced. Such a thing might be difficult to conceive, but Lévi-Strauss argues that it can be realized in the following way. A 'natural' social fact might be conceived of as being one which was universal to all societies. Clearly, there are several such 'facts' but to see what it is that is really required we must define this 'social fact' more precisely. Lévi-Strauss argues in the opening chapter of his *Elementary Structures of Kinship* that what is required is a social fact which shows the essential trait of culture, namely that it should be *arbitrary*, but which also shows the characteristic mark of nature, namely that it should be *necessary*.

The way in which he comes to do this is best explained by considering for a moment the logical and semantic difficulties surrounding the derivation of culture from nature. Nature is taken by Lévi-Strauss to be that which is common to all men and part of their hereditary endowment, it is that which all men manifest independently of the influence of society and of custom. Culture, on the other hand, is the contrary of this. It is all that is not common, all that has to be learnt, all that is dependent on social life and its collective norms. The cultural is, in other words, the contingent and the arbitrary; the natural is the necessary and the absolute. Consequently, eating, with all its Pavlovian responses, is natural in that all men do it and are lead to do it by instinct. But table manners, the mode of consumption of food, is in all societies different. Even quite subtle cultural differences, such as those distinguishing an Englishman from an American, can be readily discerned in this context, particularly in their differing use of the fork. Table manners are consequently cultural because arbitrary and contingent, salivation is natural because universal and instinctual.

So far, so good. But in searching for a common principle of culture the theorist comes across a paradox. This can be understood as follows: If a universal principle and single cause of culture can be detected in all men and all societies then it follows from the considerations above that this principle of culture must be *natural* – at least in the sense in which we have defined it. Now this is contradictory at first sight, and in fact is logically just another manifestation of the Durkheimian difficulty of reducing collective and arbitrary social norms to individual and natural causes. But Lévi-Strauss thinks that he sees in the paradox the key to its resolution. Just such a natural social fact exists for Lévi-Strauss in the field of behavioural activity called the sexual. Primary narcissism aside, sexuality, at least in its adult and genital phase, is social in the sense that it takes two. All other instincts can be gratified by the solitary says Lévi-Strauss, but not this one, – not, that is, if the race is to survive. Here, against distant strains of Darwin and Freud, Lévi-Strauss enunciates his solution to Durkheim's problem, namely that the original social fact is the avoidance of incest.

We may concede sexuality to be as social as it is natural in a very limited sense, but it can only become genuinely cultural if it is conducted on the basis of a norm or a rule – the coercive aspect of Durkheim's social fact. Clearly, sexuality by itself is insufficient, but it does provide the natural basis for Lévi-Strauss' theory. He states it as a matter of fact that the *rule* of the avoidance of incest is universal – quasi-natural – to all human societies. As one of the very few empirical generalizations made in Lévi-Strauss' work this has, not surprisingly, attracted some attention, and Edmund Leach[1] and others have denied his attestation. But whatever the empirical realities may be, it is essential to realize that Lévi-Strauss is forced to insist on this universal nature of the incest-avoidance rule in order to produce an indisputably cultural norm which is also universal and consequently 'natural' to human societies.

Of course exactly the same could be said of table manners – these too are almost unquestionably universal – but clearly the ubiquitous principle of culture must be not merely 'natural' in the sense of being common to all societies, but must in some way or another be demonstrably the structural and historical foundation on which the whole of the rest of culture rests. Table manners could not possibly be made to appear as such; the rule of the avoidance of incest might if it could be shown to be the basic element of systems of kinship and consequently of social structures at large.

The variability of the rule from one society to another unequivocally attests to its arbitrary, contingent and cultural basis, and the close relation between the rule and man's sexuality provides for Lévi-Strauss the natural basis from which society proceeds. Men remained on the level of the natural as long as they had no cultural prohibitions of this sort. But, and for whatever reasons they chose to adopt this, as soon as such a prohibion came into existence, then its structural corollary – the exchange of sisters – became a logical necessity. A renunciation of the individual's sexual right over the women of his own family immediately creates conditions favouring the creation of a social contract in that a simple solution to the problem of how to get a wife is found in exchanging sisters with other similarly placed individuals. This is the sense in which sister-exchange is the corollary of incest avoidance – if I cannot have my sister and you cannot equally have yours, there is no reason why we should not have each others'. Not only do we avoid infringing the rule against sibling incest, but we also establish a close social tie. We become relatives and we are in a position to communicate and exchange with one another on an equitable and reciprocal basis. Sister-exchange not only spells a solution to the problem of how to go about avoiding incest, it also means reciprocity and communication between wife-giving and wife-receiving groups. Since for structuralists like Lévi-Strauss reciprocating communications are the basis of social structure, and indeed a definition of it, then, clearly, this sort of social fact – the avoidance of incest – can be made to generate, both from the viewpoint of history and social structure, the key elements of society. Communication of women between groups of men comes first, both logically and historically, and establishes, as it were, the infrastructure of social communication. Then follows the communication of goods and services – *economic relations* – and words – *language.*

Here, then, is Lévi-Strauss' solution to the first part of the Durkheimian problem regarding the origin of the social fact, or, and which comes to the same thing, the reductive and causal explanation of social wholes. It is a solution to the temporal problem – to that of explaining where society came from in the first place and how a whole greater than the sum of its parts could have evolved from elements which were less than it was to become. Sexuality, an implicitly quasi-social instinct is taken as the natural spur towards the creation of culture which results, as we have seen, according to Lévi-Strauss, from the renunciation of one's own sisters and the reciprocal exchange of them with other, similarly placed men. The avoidance of incest is, quite simply, the first social fact and the foundation of culture.

A number of observations need to be made about this conclusion. First, I must point out that this idea is almost exactly the same as that put forward by Freud in his *Totem and Taboo* – a matter to which I shall return much later. Secondly, we must note the ways in which Lévi-Strauss' formulation of it differs from Freud's, even though the latter is, as we shall see, completely compatible with it. This leads us to the third important observation, namely the extent to which Lévi-Strauss' formulation of the origins of society and culture resemble those put forward by Rousseau.

Unlike Freud, both Lévi-Strauss and Rousseau appear to be arguing a social contract theory of the origins of society. Lévi-Strauss' differs from Rousseau's in detail very much, but in its general outline it is exactly similar. Both argue that a 'state of nature' might have existed before the existence of society in which men were perhaps not actually anti-social, but at least non-social. Indulgence in primal incest for Lévi-Strauss means isolation, at least compared with the situation that results from its avoidance. Men make the transition from this pre-social isolation in a state of nature to culture and society because of the advantages which the latter brings. Here an implicit functionalism exists in both Rousseau and Lévi-Strauss which suggests that men forego the state of nature and renounce incest in order to secure the benefits which accrue from the creation of kinship alliances with other groups of men, and from which, as we have seen, Lévi-Strauss sees the two other main forms of social communication, goods, services and language, proceeding. As a matter of fact, we do not necessarily have to conceive a naïve functional teleology here – that men consciously will that this should be so. All we need say, and all that Lévi-Strauss actually does say, is that, for whatever reasons men abandoned primal incest, the creation of an incest-avoidance *rule* led directly to the creation of culture and society with all its benefits. Thus the greatest of Durkheim's social facts – society – is derived from the pre-social – nature.

Here Mauss' notion of reciprocity is used by Lévi-Strauss in exactly the same way that the former had used it in his analysis of gift-giving. Reciprocity is seen as a structural principle (as well as a norm) which underlies the kinship network and whose logical derivations and corollaries determine much of what goes on in actual behaviour. But if this is so, then it clearly follows that the structural principles which Lévi-Strauss has claimed provide the *historical* basis for systems of kinship ought also to be demonstrably the *structural* basis of such systems in the present. Having once come into existence as a means of transition from nature to culture, the principle of the avoidance of incest must remain as the fundamental reality underlying all kinship systems, and not merely those of primitives. In fact we might perhaps assume that the more primitive a people the more obvious the principle, and, as we shall see, Lévi-Strauss does in fact do this. But it is clear that as a structural principle incest-avoidance and its structural corollary – reciprocal sister-exchange – must be shown to be the foundation of all systems of kinship in just the same way that Mauss showed reciprocity to underlie all systems of gift-giving.

It would not be appropriate to attempt to recount the whole of Lévi-Strauss' analysis of systems of kinship which we find in *Elementary Structures of Kinship* and elsewhere. Rather, let me make one or two brief indications which will illustrate his approach, and let the reader acquaint himself with the rest of Lévi-Strauss' material if he should wish.

Durkheim, in his *Elementary Forms of the Religious Life*, fastened on the Australian aborigines because he alleged that, as the most primitive of most other peoples, at least from the point of view of technology and culture, it was safe to assume that they might also be most primitive from the point of view of their religious institutions a point on which, incidentally, Freud agreed. Lévi-Strauss, in choosing his title for this book – *Les Structures élémentaires de la parenté* – clearly means to remind us of the title of Durkheim's work – in French, *Les Formes élémentaires de la vie religieuse* – and to suggest what I have been labouring to explain in these pages, namely, a continuity of thought between himself and the great French sociologist. In choosing to begin his analysis with Australian ethnographic examples, Lévi-Strauss is implicitly following Durkheim in the assumption that Australian aborigines are in some way or another closer to the origins of culture in their systems of kinship than other peoples might be – that these systems are, in a word, more 'elementary'.

A common type of kinship system met with in Australia is what is known as the marriage-class system. The well-known Aranda, for example, operate an eight-part example of such a system, and the Kariera, whom we shall be looking at, do so with four classes. The Kariera explain their kinship system as follows:

Everybody belongs to one of four classes (for convenience I will not give their proper names but call them 1, 2, 3, and 4). Membership of these four marriage classes is determined as follows: A man in 1 marries a woman in 2, and the children are 3. A man in 2 marries a woman in 1, and the children are 4. A man in 4 marries a woman in 3, and the children are 2. A man in 3 marries a woman in 4, and the children are 1.

The system is perhaps easier to understand if represented by a diagram (Fig. 1 A), in which double lines represent marriage, and single lines descent. The diagram only represents the marriage choices of men, not those of women. Hence to make sense of it one must always begin with a man in one group who marries a woman in another and whose children are allocated to a third.

This does not appear to have much to do with incest-avoidance, or with exchanging sisters. However, if we look at a geneological representation of the marriage rule (Fig 1 B), we see that it clearly does. If we look at the system of marriage-classes from the point of view of any man in class 1, we see that what the marriage rule effectively says (expressed in *negative* terms) is that a man in 1 may *not* marry his mother, or anyone else in her class (the 4s), including his sister's children (who are also 4s). Neither may he marry his daughters, or his father's sisters (the 3s), nor his own sisters, nor his father's father's sisters (the 1s). There remains only one group into which he may marry legitimately – the 2s.

Here the rule of the avoidance of incest has been extended into a rule of exogamy which effectively results in dividing the society into halves, or moieties, each of which is a patrilineal descent group (1s and 3s, 2s and 4s), and which, in each generation, exchange sisters between them. Thus for every woman lost by the 1s, a woman should be returned from the 2s, and so on. The Kariera four-part marriage-class system can thus be seen as no more than an established system of sister-exchange between two groups of men, conceived on the basis of the avoidance of incest with closely related females. Much the same sort of remarks can be made about the Aranda eight-part system, or indeed, any such system operating on similar lines.

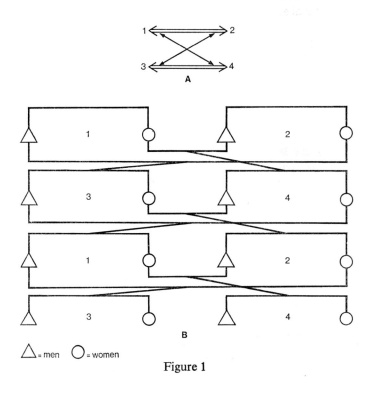

Figure 1

Such systems are based on what Lévi-Strauss terms *restricted exchange*. This applies to systems in which the 'wife-givers' are the same as the 'wife-takers', as we have seen the Kariera to be. The other alternative is what he calls *generalized exchange*. This is a system where such direct reciprocity does not exist. An extreme case of generalized exchange is provided by our own society in which no positive prescriptive marriage rules exist. This results in a random pattern of marriage choices which, assuming monogamy and the avoidance of incest, results in a generalized exchange of sisters so that, on average and in general, women are evenly distributed between groups of men.

The restricted exchange system of the Kariera type might be characterized as *mechanical*, as opposed to ours, which might be termed *statistical*. An analogy might make the relation clear. Suppose that one were making a very small cherry cake for just four persons, and that one possessed only four cherries – it being very important that each person should in fact get a cherry in his slice. The obvious way to proceed would be to add the cherries at the last moment before baking the cake and to place them in it in a regular and pre-determined way so that on cutting it one could assume that each person would have the essential cherry somewhere in his slice. If, however, one were making a very large cake for a large number of persons one would be much more likely to merely add a large quantity of cherries and stir for a while, assuming that, on average and in general and all the other things being equal, everyone stood an equal chance of getting some cherries in their slice. The former possibility corresponds to a Kariera-type system in which women are 'mechanically' placed in pre-determined groups of men. The latter corresponds to a 'statistical' system of generalized exchange, such as exists in our own society. In both cases women are evenly distributed around the system and reciprocity is maintained even though in the statistical and generalized system it is guaranteed by the random pattern of choices rather than by direct mechanical reciprocity as in the restricted situation. In both cases the exchange of sisters fulfils the vital structural function which Lévi-Strauss alleges is the foundation of culture, namely the establishment of systems of communication between sister-exchanging groups of men.

In this way Lévi-Strauss argues that the basic principle from which he was able to derive the creation of culture can still be seen to be operative in the system which is structurally fundamental to all others – namely, kinship.

Totemism

But this will not fully elucidate what I suggested might be seen as the second part of the Durkheimian problem regarding the reductive and causal explanation of the origin of the social fact. The reader will recall that this was a question of the structural and synchronic relation between social facts and that which makes them up; a problem which is otherwise known to sociological theory as that of Individualism versus Holism.

One or two observations need to be made upon this difficulty before we look at Lévi-Strauss' attempted resolution of it. The first is that it is analogous to the problem which we have just considered – the explanation of the historical origin of culture – and so logically forms an indivisible part of it. Secondly, we must recall that, in Durkheim's case, this difficulty had an indelible *psychological* stamp. In the present, Durkheim understood culture – or the sum total of social facts, or *conscience collective*, as he in fact called it – as being contained in a system of collective representations. These were inscribed on the mind of the individual from birth onwards by socialization and came to provide the psychological and causal basis of normal behaviour (that is, behaviour in accordance with norms). Finally, we should bear in mind that although analogous to the question of the origins of the social fact and allied to it, this problem is quite independent in that what has been appealed to in order to explain the origin of society in time cannot necessarily be expected to provide a full explanation of its persistence into the present. The fact that incest-avoidance and sister-exchange can perhaps be shown to be basic to systems of kinship, and systems of kinship basic to culture, does not in itself explain *why* men maintain the avoidance of incest and systems of culture in existence. For this, a quite different sort of explanation is required.

Lévi-Strauss' response to this difficulty is nowhere better seen than in his works on totemism, and in particular in the opening chapters of *The Savage Mind* – a book which is, in many ways, the most difficult of all his output, and must, to the reader unprepared by an existing knowledge of anthropological and sociological theory (not to mention an acquaintance with the works of Sartre), be largely incomprehensible at a first reading. As a matter of fact, the ideas put forward in this book are not really difficult to understand, and I intend to attempt an exegesis of it in the last part of this chapter and in the next. But in order to comprehend fully the significance of Lévi-Strauss' theory of totemism it is first necessary to recall briefly what Durkheim had to say on this matter.

In his *Primitive Classification*, to which we have already referred, Durkheim encapsulated his explanation of the curious phenomenon of totemism in the remark to the effect that 'the first logical categories are social categories'.[2]

Totemism is a system of nomenclature by means of which individual human beings, as well as groups of people, are given the names of natural objects – usually plants and animals, but also occasionally those of geographical features, meteorological conditions, diseases, and so forth. Along with the name of the natural species goes an elaborate array of rituals and prohibitions, and notions of mystical union or magical complicity link the individual concerned with the totem object. Thus, if it is a question of an animal species, for example, rituals guaranteeing the successful reproduction of the animals concerned may be encumbent on the members of the totemic community, prohibitions against eating the species in question may be in force, and ritual dances and magical festivals linked with the totem will probably punctuate the life of the persons concerned.

Durkheim's theory, as we find it in *Primitive Classification* and *Elementary Forms of the Religious Life*, is entirely in harmony with his general theoretical position. First comes the *conscience collective* which lays down a social classification – the social structure (in this case, exogamous clans) – then this social classification is projected, as it were, on to nature, and natural classifications – species of plants and animals – are identified with it.

Lévi-Strauss' approach, as we find it in his *Totemism* and opening chapters of *The Savage Mind*, is exactly the reverse. In so many words he maintains that the first social categories are logical categories, in that primitive men, like civilized ones, classify and order their experience of natural phenomena spontaneously and frequently irrespective of the economic and social value of the objects classified. 'Classifying', remarks Lévi-Strauss, 'as opposed to not classifying, has a value of its own, whatever form the classification may take.'[3] Taxonomy, he argues, is the first stage in the establishment of science; and magic, as an explanatory and practical system, can only be distinguished from it in that 'magic postulates a complete and all-embracing determinism',[4] which presumably science has the good sense, or bad luck, to avoid. 'Both science and magic however require the same sort of mental operations.'[5]

This sort of statement is in one sense vaguely reminiscent of Comte; but the exact contrary in another. It is reminiscent in that Lévi-Strauss appears to be talking in terms of a universal psychological propensity on the part of the human race, both savage and civilized, *to know*. Comte, too, in his belief on an inevitable ever-on-and-upward search for positive truth had a very similar idea. But where this differs completely is in Comte's isolation of the scientific thought of positivism to the third and final stage of human evolution. Lévi-Strauss, by contrast, appears to deny the exclusiveness of positivism to modern science and purports to find it underlying the processes of primitive thought. The research scientist and the shaman are here represented as differing not by virtue of one of them belonging in the gloom of animist superstition and the other in supreme and refulgent positivism, but rather as differing from one another 'not so much in kind as in the different types of phenomena to which they are applied'[6] These overtones of Comte, and this apparent complete departure from the Law of the Three Stages are of great significance in resolving the Durkheimian difficulty of the structural origin of the social fact, as we shall see in a moment.

One of the most important distinctions between primitive and modern thought is brought out by Lévi-Strauss in his use of the analogy of *bricolage*. The *bricoleur*, who appears to be a peculiarly French, and, I suspect, dying species, is a sort of handyman who will use whatever comes to hand to do a job by inspired 'ad-hocism' rather than with purpose-made parts. He is the sort of repairman who can always make do with something he has with him rather than the replacement listed in the catalogue. This use of a set of existing means for the service of new ends is what Lévi-Strauss means by *bricolage*, and he maintains that it is an important aspect of primitive thought. Whereas modern science uses purpose-made concepts and explanatory systems (above all, mathematics), primitive thought uses pre-existing objects to serve new intellectual purposes. Totemism is just such a system of thought, and one of the most important examples of cerebral *bricolage*. But before we go on to see how this is so, let us first digress for a moment into an area without recourse to which we cannot get far in understanding Lévi-Strauss – namely structural linguistics.

This use of existing elements in a new way – *bricolage* – transforms the elements of thought which it uses into *signs*. The sign, says Lévi-Strauss, 'lies halfway between perception and conception'. It is something which represents a concept, or an idea, but is not in itself a concept or an idea. Similarly, it is derived from perceptions of the world – it *is* something – but, in the new use to which it is put it is *not* that thing. A red traffic-light *is* a red traffic-light, no doubt about that. A red traffic-light *means* 'Stop!' As a *sign* the traffic-light lies midway between the physical perception –red light – and the concept 'Stop!'

The notion of the sign was first fully developed in structural linguistics by Ferdinand de Saussure in his classic *Cours de linguistique générale*. As far as the linguistic sign is concerned, de Saussure had two most important things to say. First, he created a distinction between *the signified* and *the signifier*, or semantic content and linguistic sign; and secondly, he maintained that the link between the signified and the signifier was *arbitrary*. In the case of the word 'apple', a more or less spherical, arboreal and sweet-tasting fruit growing in temperate climates is the signified – the semantic content – and the speech sound represented by the letters a-p-p-l-e is the signifier, or *sign*. We can readily see that de Saussure is right about maintaining the arbitrary nature of the association of the two because we know that some people say '*pomme*'. If there were a necessary connection between the idea 'apple' and the word 'apple' our French cousins would not be at liberty to say '*pomme*'. The linguistic sign, in other words, is arbitrary; it stands for something by convention and common usage, not by necessity.

The tendency of *bricolage* then, in primitive thought, is to transform ends into means and *vice versa*, in that existing ends – animal species classified as such for their own sake – become the means of social classification – totemism – an operation which turns these animal species into signs in that what they denote is now no longer simply themselves but something else. Similarly, a plant or animal species, a means to an ordering of nature, now becomes in totemism an end in itself. The signifier, the species itself, changes its meaning – it's signified – and comes to stand for something quite different in a quite different system of orderings.

Thus Lévi-Strauss argues, contrary to Durkheim, that the existing natural classifications – species – are turned by totemism's *bricolage* into social classification – totemic clans. Here the natural species play the rôle of the signifiers and the clans the rôle of the signified in what we may call the language of totemism.

We have already seen Lévi-Strauss talking about kinship systems in terms of communication. It should now come as no surprise to see him talking about totemism as a language, another system of communication, but one in which the 'words' are natural species, and the semantic content social groups. The function of the communication system of kinship was, as we saw, that of creating links between otherwise discreet groups of men. The function of the quasi-linguistic system of totemism is that of representing both to the native himself and to outsiders the structure of his own society and the nature of his own social identity.

Yet if the link between signified and signifier is as arbitrary as we have seen de Saussure maintaining it to be, then it follows that other possibilities may exist. Indeed they do. Lévi-Strauss suggests in the pages of *The Savage Mind* that a completely inverted system of signification is possible. Totemism tends to make groups of people appear like animal species. Now the distinguishing characteristic of animal species is that they mate only among themselves. If totemic clans really were like animal species they would be endogamous and one would marry one's clan 'sisters'. In fact, totemic clans are exogamous, and marriage with a clan 'sister' is regarded as incestuous. Hence, the tendency of the clan name to isolate and mark off a group of people from all other groups on the basis of an analogy with the way in which animal species are distinguished from one another is balanced by a marriage rule – exogamy – which has the effect of integrating that same quasi-specific group into the wider structure of society. We *are* Night-Hawks, but we *marry* Owls. Our name distinguishes us and sets us apart, but our kinship links integrate us into other totemic groups.

But from the point of view of the function of such a system of nomenclature and marriage rule the opposite arrangement might work just as well. We might have endogamous groups, that is, in-marrying groups, which would consequently have no kinship links with the wider society, and instead of a name which isolates us and sets us apart, one which integrates us and provides the connections with other groups not forthcoming from our marriage rule. Such an arrangement does in fact exist and is known as the caste system. Here endogamous caste groups are integrated into society by economic interdependence and are represented by a cultural naming system, broadly that of occupation. This latter feature contrasts with the natural system of nomenclature found in totemism. Where totemism uses the name of a natural species to distinguish and isolate social groups, caste uses occupational distinctions and the division of labour to integrate such groups. Where totemism insists on clan exogamy to provide for social links with the rest of society, caste demands endogamy in order to maintain the distinct identity and the social definition of the occupational group. Caste commensality and notions of ritual pollution represent the structural inversion of the totemic eating prohibitions. We, the barber caste, marry the daughters of other barbers, but we cut the hair of the leather-workers who, in turn, provide us with the straps which we need to sharpen our razors, and so on.

Any 'language' like totemism or caste must perform two social functions: it must integrate society and consolidate it, but it must also discriminate and subdivide it into the necessary sub-groupings which everyday life makes desirable. Caste and totemism each perform this function, but by totally opposite means. The signifiers are complete opposites, but the signified, as a system of social relation-ships, is structurally closely analogous.

Before going on to consider Lévi-Strauss' theory of myth, it would be as well to pause for a moment and reflect on the theoretical significance of this use of a linguistic analogy in dealing with the mysteries of totemism. A first observation which we might make is that language, considered as a systematic entity, a system of lexical and syntactical norms, is a highly Durkheimian phenomenon. It is what Durkheim would have termed the system of linguistic *représentations collectives*. De Saussure is entirely in agreement with this view of language, defining it as 'a social pro-duct of the linguistic faculty, and a system of necessary connections adopted by the body of society' – Durkheim would have said, *conscience collective* – 'to permit the exercise of that faculty in the individual members'.[7]

It is obvious to everyone that language is a collective entity determined by conventions and consensus and taught by socialization. Yet the significance of de Saussure to Lévi-Strauss' methodology is exactly analogous to that of Mauss. Lévi-Strauss uses structural linguistics to provide exactly the same sort of remedy to the log-jam of Durkheim's functionalist holism in respect of the structural origins of society as we have seen him do with regard to the problems of the origins of social wholes in time.

The importance of Mauss was that his analysis, particularly in *The Gift*, allowed us to move from the purely conscious normative consensus to the structural and unconscious system of communication. For Mauss it was the implicit logic of the principle of reciprocity that mattered, rather than the conscious norm. An exactly analogous situation exists with regard to de Saussure's linguistics.

The Durkheimian aspects of language are so obvious that they can hardly take us any distance at all towards understanding it. Everybody knows the conscious norms – the rules of grammar and semantics – they must do, at least implicitly, in order to be able to speak at all. The significance of de Saussure's contribution was that it focused attention on the unconscious and purely structural aspects of language and developed a structural technique for analysing it. We have already encountered one of the major aspects of this technique – the definition of the arbitrary nature of the linguistic sign. If we follow developments in structural linguistics for a moment, and especially with regard to this aspect of language – the sign – we shall begin to see exactly what sort of unconscious structural principles de Saussure and his followers claim to have found. Among the most important of these followers as far as Lévi-Strauss is concerned is the modern structural linguist Roman Jakobson. If we look at his approach to the linguistic sign, considered merely as a pattern of speech sounds, we shall see that he introduces a mode of structural analysis which has made a great impact on Lévi-Strauss. Jakobson proposed binary oppositions as the basis of the organization of distinctive features at the phonetic level of language. If we ignore the semantic level for a moment and look solely at the linguistic sign – the speech sounds, or phonemes, of which a word is composed – we find according to Jakobson that:

all differences of phonemes in any language can be resolved into simple and indecomposable binary oppositions.[8]

These binary oppositions, or distinctive features, are simple Yes/No choices based on nine 'sonority features' and three 'tonality features' of language, themselves ultimately determined by the physiology and functioning of the larynx, nasal cavities, mouth, teeth etc. Thus, according to Jakobson, when we hear the phonemes of the word 'cat', for instance, we distinguish them on the basis of whether they are compact or diffuse, consonantal or non-consonantal, nasal or oral, strident or mellow, and so on. He says that:

. . . in reducing the phonemic information contained in the sequence to the smallest number of alternatives, we find the most economical and consequently the optimal solution: the minimum number of the simplest operations that would suffice to encode and decode the whole message.[9]

An interesting application of this idea to an old controversy is the Jakobsonian explanation of the extreme commonness of the word 'mama' in human languages signifying 'mother'. Now, no science based on the principle of the arbitrary nature of the linguistic sign could possibly maintain that there was an intrinsic connection between the idea 'mother' and the word 'mama'. Nor would a Diffusionist or Evolutionist explanation do. Jakobson's explanation is that quite simply the phonemes /m/ and /a/ are two of the simplest that can exist. The open vocalizing tract of /a/ contrasts with the completely closed /m/, the vowel with the consonant, the strident tonality feature with the mellow, and so on. /m/ tends to be a natural sound of contentment, /a/, a natural cry of protest. When run together and repeated we have a genuine word, since it is the element of redundancy in the repetition of the two sounds that signifies that we are hearing not just two random and contradictory sounds but four significant phonemes. Seen in the light of these considerations, the ubiquity of words like 'mama' is not really surprising; it results according to structural linguistics from common structural and physiological processes present in all human beings and in all languages.

Jakobson and his associates claim to have found such binary oppositions not only underlying phonemic structure but also as a major feature operating at the level of words and sentences. Indeed, the assertion that such tendencies to construct binary oppositions are fundamental to thought is as important a part of Lévi-Strauss' structuralism as is his notion of the arbitrary nature of systems of signification taken from de Saussure, or that of the structural principles underlying reciprocity and communication borrowed from Mauss.

The importance of this idea stems from the fact that, for Lévi-Strauss, approaches like that of Jakobson provide some insight into the process of thought underlying mental structures like totemism and myth. This allows us to circumvent the difficulty which Durkheim found himself in when confronted by the demand for a final explanation for the origins of mental structures. As we have seen, Durkheim made the excuse that these were inexplicable because of an irrational and collective origin. For Lévi-Strauss, however, this is not the case. The ultimate origins of the categories of thought which are the basis of totemism, and indeed, of the whole of culture, or the *conscience collective* as Durkheim would have called it, are neither irrational, nor collective, but rational and individual. Just as Jakobson attempts to show that the choice of phonemes in a language can be reduced to a simple set of logical operations, given the parameters of the system of voice articulation, so Lévi-Strauss assumes that the complete range of collective codes which make up culture can be reduced in principle at least to a set of rational, but unconscious mental operations. The collective aspect of these cultural phenomena is to be explained by reference to the fact that all men have similar minds, at least as far as structure is concerned, and hence collective aspects of culture reflect the broadly similar mass of individual psyches.

The solution to Durkheim's second problem then, that of the apparently irreducible and inexplicable nature of the social fact considered from the point of view of its origins in the members of a society, is solved by recourse to a model of the mind which sees it as functioning on the basis of universally shared, rational but unconscious processes. Now culture is no longer greater than the sum of its parts, but can be reduced ultimately to the physiology of the brain.

In this respect culture is reduced to nature in just the same way that we saw Lévi-Strauss reduce it in the case of the historical origin of the social whole. There a natural tendency – human sexuality – was made to result in a universal avoidance of incest which became the first social fact, and linked nature (sexuality) with culture (prohibitive rules). Here an exactly analogous type of explanation is suggested in which nature – now understood as the functioning and physiology of the brain as a natural object – is seen to be the origin of culture – collective systems of categories of thought – which underlie codes of communication like totemism in just the same sort of way that the operations of the brain in creating binary oppositions of speech sounds is seen as underlying the purely cultural expressions which we call words.

Myth

But this sort of explanation is not only the basis of Lévi-Strauss' approaches to kinship and totemism. It is also fundamental to the way in which he deals with a human phenomenon hardly less mystifying than totemism, namely myth. Lévi-Strauss starts his analysis of myth with a simple definition; a myth is something which tells a story. It is an anecdote. Unlike poetry, where the individual word is all-important, in myth what matters is the story, not the word. Hence myths, according to Lévi-Strauss, unlike poems, translate well.[10] Indeed, he maintains they translate with more or less no loss of value whereas a poem will of necessity lose some of its significance when the sound of the words in which it is expressed, the 'matter' of the signification, is translated into some other 'matter' (some other system of phonemes) which does not have the same phonetic characteristics. The fact that this is not the case with myth is all-important, for it focuses attention on that aspect of mythology which is essential, namely that the 'matter' of the myth, its primary substance of signification, is not rooted in the word combinations in which it is first expressed but rather is based in other relations, in structures of a higher order.

Hence, myths consist, according to Lévi-Strauss, essentially in telling stories. They relate a sequence of events whose importance lies in the events themselves and in the details which accompany them. Thus myths are always open to re-expression, and particularly lend themselves to translation. In other words, myths can be retold *in other words* – they can be paraphrased and condensed, expanded and elaborated.

This is all in strict and absolute contrast to poetry, which lends itself above all to written literature. In the poem words may not be substituted or altered at will. What is essential is that the words originally chosen should be the words preserved, and a poem once completed takes on a rigidity and perfection unknown to the world of myth.

It follows from what has been said that linguistics, the science of language on the level of the phoneme and the word, is inapplicable to myth. Myth as Lévi-Strauss has defined it exists on a higher level of organization. Its basic significant units are not phonemes, or whole words, but rather the phrase and the sentence. Furthermore, the phrase and the sentence are considered from the point of view of their content, the ideas which they convey rather than from that of their phonetic or morphological aspects. This content, following the example of de Saussure's phonetics, is broken up into irreducible 'atoms' of the complex molecular structure of myths, for as I have already said, to go to a lower level of organization would be to go back to the phoneme and the word, in short, to de Saussure's linguistics. The study of myth should be, according to Lévi-Strauss, an autonomous science, irreducible to others.

As I have said above, the significant units of myths are phrases and sentences which are the fundamental particles of the anecdote which the myth essentially is. Clearly, the study of myth is the study of the structural inter-relations of these fundamental particles or 'mythemes' as Lévi-Strauss calls them, using this term to underline the parallel with the phoneme of structural linguistics.

The signs of the myth – the mythemes – are as arbitrary as the signs of language, and as such have value only in terms of their inter-relations.[11] Like linguistics, the structural study of myth is the study of the transformations of the sign. As de Saussure had said in the analogous case of linguistics:

for the science of language, it will be sufficient always to state the transformations of sounds and to calculate their effects.[12]

But whereas linguistics studies the transformations of sounds, of the *tranche de sonorité* as de Saussure called it, the science of myth studies the transformations of mythemes and the discourse of myths. But if myths, because they tell stories, are closely related to history and literature, then it is also true that, because they have a structure, they are closely related to music. This analogy of myth with music is something which Lévi-Strauss makes a great deal of in the opening pages of his major work on myths, *Mythologiques*.

The relevance of music to myth becomes clear if we notice the following points. In his structural linguistics, de Saussure had distinguished between the *synchronic* and the *diachronic*. The diachronic is the dimension of time and of progression, of change and development. The synchronic is a dimension at right angles to this and represents simultaneity rather than progression, space rather than time, system rather than change. In linguistics, the synchronic dimension of language is that which represents it at every instant as a complete and coherent system. The diachronic in language represents it as changing and evolving in time as it is actually spoken. In music, the diachronic is the melody, the synchronic is the harmony. Myths, by their very nature, must unfold diachronically, one must begin at the beginning and go on to the end. One event in the story must give way to another, just as one phoneme is followed by another in speech. Unlike music, the signifiers of myth cannot be sounded simultaneously, giving the harmony to the melody. This would mean telling two stories at once, which would obscure the sense. But, in two quite different ways, myth does have a synchronic dimension. First, the synchronic dimension exists within the myth, since if the myth is a series of structurally related mythemes – mythemes related by grammar and syntax in a diachronic sense, into an anecdote – it is clear that they may equally well be linked in a synchronic, simultaneous sense by memory and recollection. Hence one mythemic transformation at the beginning of the myth may 'harmonize' with another at the end, and indeed, only derive its significance from this relation. In a second sense, mythemes may 'harmonize' with those in other myths, just as in music, where harmony may be within the same melodic line (as in the *concertante* style), or between more than one melodic line (as in fugal, polyphonic forms). We shall meet examples of this below.

The second main point we must notice in working out the significance of the analogy between music and mythology is that myths, like music, make use of arbitrary transformations. Thus a composer such as Bach in his *Art of Fugue* may take a theme, a simple melody, and then transform it in accordance with quite arbitrary usages; for example, he may turn it upside-down, turn it back-to-front, combine it with its own inverted mirror-image, and so on. In just the same way a myth may select a simple 'theme', such as that for instance which deals with the origin of tobacco, and subject it to arbitrary transformations in just the same way. Thus the theme may be inverted, reversed, reversed and inverted, combined with another, varied, amplified, simplified, and so on. Furthermore, besides these 'polyphonic' transformations, the myth will inevitably use the basic element of musical form, repetition and variation.

Since the mythemes or fragments of the myth are arbitrary and are located in an arbitrary time, in the time of 'Once upon a time' and in the world of unaccountable, chance and supernatural happenings, it is clear that commonsensicality and the every-day connotation of things is quite irrelevant. Myth does not convey commonsensical information, it is not for practical purposes. It serves no utilitarian end whatsoever, and conveys no information about the everyday world. Nor is it necessarily morally or politically pedagogic. In the Bororo myths dealt with in *The Raw and the Cooked* for instance, the myths, counter to the moral code of Bororo society, praise incestuous unions and reward the guilty by punishing the offended.[13] In absence of a utilitarian purpose it would be tempting to see myths as decorative. But nothing could be further from the essential truth, for myth, unlike poetical conceits, swear words and oaths does not function as an elaboration, or a decorous addition to every-day speech. Rather it is a field of discourse quite alone in its native setting, indeed, quite often separated by native practitioners into a special, sacred context. To consider it as a purely gratuitous, decorative activity of the primitive mind would of necessity be to return to the child-savage theories of anthropologists such as Lévy-Bruhl. On the contrary, myth in reality is extremely purposeful. The question of the real meaning of myth is one which must be postponed until the end of this chapter, but for the time being suffice it to say that myth is a means of structuring and ordering reality, a means of understanding it in the sense that totemism, for instance, is a means of understanding to the people who practice it. Whereas totemism, ritual, or modes of cooking may be seen as ways of ordering and classifying natural phenomena and men, myth may be seen as exactly the same undertaking with the difference that myth is above all an ordering of concepts and an expression in anecdotes, since unlike these other examples it is limited to realization in words alone.

It is not my purpose to justify or criticize the origins or the form of presentation of the myths in *Mythologiques*. What interests us in the methodological significance of what Lévi-Strauss has written, and this is bound to concentrate our attention on the consideration of his method rather than the quality of the original texts which could only be investigated by studies in the field and in manuscript sources which the present writer has not the competence to undertake.

The terrain of myth, as Lévi-Strauss says, is round, or, more precisely, spherical. It looks much the same from any point of view and lacks a clear point on entry or a definite place of culmination. Rather than relate entire myths and their analysis as Lévi-Strauss does, it will probably be better merely to exemplify some of the transformations that he isolates and leave the reader to pursue the question of their relation to the original myth and cultural context. Usually, the form in which Lévi-Strauss presents the myths is that of a full narrative account to begin with, and then a simplified, schematized system of mythemes in opposition. The case of myths 23, 24 and 26 will furnish a good example. We may summarize them roughly thus:

M_{23} One day a woman and her husband went to catch parakeets The man climbed a tree containing several nests and threw down thirty or so fledglings to his wife. He noticed that she gobbled them up. Seized with fear, he caught hold of a larger bird and, as he threw it down, called out, 'Here comes a fledgling, but look out it can fly.'

The woman ran after the bird, and the man took advantage of the situation to climb down and run away: he was afraid she might eat him too. But his wife went after him, caught up with him, and killed him. Then she cut off his head, which she put in a bag, and feasted on the rest of the body until her stomach was full.

She had scarcely returned to the village when she felt thirsty. Before going to the drinking pool, which was some distance away, she forbade her five children to touch the bag. But the youngest immediately looked inside and called the others, who recognized their father. The whole village was now informed, and everybody took fright and ran away. except the children. When the mother, on her return, was surprised to find the village empty, they explained that the villagers had left after insulting them, having fled through shame at their own spitefulness.

The woman was indignant and, wishing to avenge her children, went after the villagers. She caught up with them, killed a number of them, and devoured the bodies there and then. The same process was repeated several times. Terrified by these bloody comings and goings, the children wanted to escape. 'Do not try to run away', said the mother, lest I eat you, too.' The children implored her. 'No, don't be afraid', she replied. No one was able to kill her, and the rumour soon spread that she was a jaguar-woman.

The children secretly dug a pit, which they covered with branches. They took flight when their mother announced to them that their turn had now come to be eaten. She rushed after them and fell into the trap. The children went to ask help from Carancho who advised them to hollow out a tree trunk and hide inside with him. The jaguar-woman tried to tear the tree with her claws but they remained caught in the wood, so that Carancho was able to come out and kill her. Her corpse was burned on a woodpile. Four or five days later a plant sprang up from the ashes. This was the first appearance of tobacco.

M_{24} There was a woman who was a sorceress. She defiled caraguata plants (a *Bromeliacex*, the central leaves of which are specked with red at the base) with menstrual blood then served the plants to her husband as food. The husband, having been told about this by her son, announced that he was going into the bush to look for honey.

After knocking the soles of his leather sandals together to find honey more easily, he discovered a hive at the bottom of a tree and a snake nearby. He kept the pure honey for his son, and for his wife prepared a mixture composed of honey and the flesh of snake embryos taken from the belly of the one he had killed.

No sooner had the woman begun to eat her portion than her body started to itch. As she scratched herself, she announced to her husband that she was about to devour him. He ran away and climbed to the top of a tree where there was a parrot's nest. He kept the ogress quiet temporarily by throwing to her the three nestlings, one after the other. While she was chasing the largest which was trying to flutter away from her, the husband ran off in the direction of a pit that he himself had dug for the purpose of catching game. He avoided the pit, but the woman fell into it and was killed.

The man filled in the hole and kept watch over it. An unknown plant eventually sprouted there. Out of curiosity the man dried the leaves in the sun; at nightfall he smoked in great secret. His companions caught him at it and asked what he was doing. Thus it was that men came to have tobacco.

M_{26} The men were returning from the hunt, and, as is customary, they whistled to their wives to come to meet them and help them to transport the game.

It so happened that a woman called Aturuaroddo picked up a piece of a boa that her husband had killed; the blood coming from the snake's flesh penetrated into her and fertilized her.

While still in the womb, the 'son of the blood' conversed with his mother and suggested that he should help her to gather wild fruit. He emerged in the form of a snake, climbed a tree, picked the fruit, and threw it down for his mother to collect. She tried to run away from him, but he caught up with her and returned to the shelter of the womb.

The woman was horrified and confided in her elder brothers who organized an ambush. As soon as the snake emerged and climbed the tree, the mother ran away; when he came down to go after her, the brothers killed him.

The body was burned on a woodpile, and from the ashes sprouted the urucu bush, the resin tree, tobacco, maize and cotton.[14]

Broken down into mythemes and schematized these three myths produce the opposite 'score' which I reproduce from Lévi-Strauss' book, and which represents a simplified version of myths 23, 24 and 26. It does not contain all the mythemes in these myths, but only some of them. However, those that it does contain may be seen as the most fundamental, as providing the essential framework of the myths.

When set out in this way the relation of each myth to the others becomes clear as a system of transformations of basic themes. Thus in a diachronic manner all three myths undergo, each in its own way, a set of transformations which results in an initial theme (a man married to the spouse of a jaguar, a mother whose son was a snake) going through a series of stages to end as the discovery of tobacco. In a synchronic sense, in the dimension of simultaneities, these stages of transformation themselves appear as transformations

of one another. Furthermore, it is most important to note that these
synchronic transformations, these 'harmonies' in the myths, operate
on the principle of uniformity or opposition. Hence the first
mytheme of M_{23} harmonizes uniformally with that of M_{24}, whereas they both contrast with that of M_{26}, which is the opposite:

$M_{23}-$ M_{24} — A husband ($\triangle$, affinal relationship)	has a wife jaguar	destructive through the mouth	of a husband who has climbed a tree
M_{26} — A mother ($\bigcirc$, blood relationship)	has a son snake	protective through the vagina	of a son who has climbed a tree

$M_{23}-$ M_{24} — looking for animals (birds)	that the wife ought not to eat (but does);	disjunction through the agency of the husband
M_{26} — looking for vegetable food (fruit)	that the mother ought to eat (but does not);	disjunction through the agency of the mother

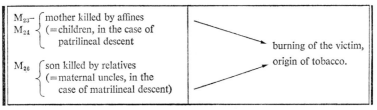

$M_{23}-$
M_{24}　A husband to a wife of a jaguar

M_{26} A mother to a son who is a snake

The principle of contrast continues throughout the myths until the
last transformations, where all oppositions are resolved and all three
myths achieve uniformity:

M_{23} Burning of the victim,
M_{24} origin of tobacco.
M_{26}

Mythologiques is a vast work, and I cannot possibly attempt to reproduce anything like the whole of Lévi-Strauss' vastly complex method of myth analysis. Suffice it to say that these particular myths, although chosen at random, and although no better than any others as an example of Lévi-Straussian myth analysis, do exhibit characteristics of myth which are essentially structural and quasi-musical. The heavy emphasis on music throughout this section of this chapter is justifiable by reference to Lévi-Strauss' own lengthy remarks on the subject in the 'Overture' to the whole work, the concert form of volume one, and his remarks in volume four. The real significance of this musical analogy will only become clear later, when we discuss Lévi-Strauss' analysis of myths in the light of his debt to Freud. For the time being, let us merely provisionally conclude that these three myths, considered in this way, do appear to exhibit some interesting structural correlations.

But, as well as pursuing the similarities to musical counterpoint, it is also necessary to keep in mind the differences that the counterpoint of myths reveals. Myths, after all, are not really played simultaneously in carefully devised harmony. The visible counterpoint is entirely the result of the work of the analyst. In complete contrast to music, the different parts which 'harmonize' in the synchronic may not even be found in the same geographical locality. They will probably correspond to differing versions of a myth held by different peoples speaking different languages, and having different social structures. Nor is the logic of the transformations so obvious in all cases. The mathematics of Bach's fugues may not be obvious to a listener, but to a person able to read music, they appear pretty obvious on the page. This is not the case with all the myths found in *Mythologiques*.

If we are to believe Lévi-Strauss, so obscure is the logic of mythological thought that it remained largely unnoticed until he discovered it. And even then, it appears to require immense efforts of analysis before the separate mythemes can be displayed and opposed. Finally, the process of analysis seems highly biased and particular. It chooses some elements and disregards others, it concentrates on the bare framework of the anecdote at some points, but relies on the significance of details at others. In some places it takes the meaning at face-value, in others it searches deeper for inner cultural correspondences and symbolisms. In short, the parallel with music can look very perplexing and not at all obvious at times.

Yet it remains nevertheless true that myths like those in my example can be analysed in the way that we have seen, and that the resulting 'score' does seem to relate to an essential reality which exists quite independently of the mind of the analyst. However different the mythological and musical situations may appear, the fact remains that the three myths taken in my example can be seen in the way Lévi-Strauss has presented them, and indeed, one may go further and say that this presentation does in fact reveal their essential form.

What is clear is that myths make use of logical inversion, reversal of events, and an apparently absurd array of subsidary details. As I pointed out above, their meaning is not to be found in any obvious didactic purpose, either moral or philosophical. Discourse that can apparently reverse the chain of events, or invert its logic at will cannot be said to qualify as what we would normally call rational conceptual thinking. If it remains didactic in a more subtle way then it is didactic by very different means. Yet it is equally clear that it is not irrational; or rather, this becomes clear on the evidence of what Lévi-Strauss purports to have shown in his book. This is that the discourse of myths does possess a principle of reasoning and that it deals in concepts, but whereas our familiar, commonsense, every-day reasoning proceeds under the rubric of a conventional, syllogistic logic, the discourse of myths proceeds by means of quite different logical principles which appear to be arbitrary or capricious in their effect. This non-commonsensical, apparently irrational aspect of myths means that inevitably ordinary methods of literary comprehension will be inappropriate in attempting to understand them.

According to Lévi-Strauss the essential intelligibility of myths is comparable to that of music. If myths are like music in their form as I have been trying to suggest, then it follows that they may be like it in terms of their content, by which I mean that myths may resemble music on a subjective level as well as on an objective and formal one. Music is obviously a question of relations of relations, the signifiers of musical discourse signifying only their own relationships as is clearly seen by the fact that a tune may remain recognizably the same even though it has been transposed into another key – the actual notes being different but their relation remaining the same. In listening to music, according to Lévi-Strauss, pure systems of relations – musical themes – originally created by the purely formal functioning of the mind of the composer are reintegrated into the formal activity of the mind of the listener. This formal activity has a double valency in Lévi-Strauss' view. First a cultural one, in that a set of culturally determined formal properties (e.g. the tempered scale) are compared and contrasted with their formal articulation in the particular piece of music; and secondly a natural one in that certain 'visceral' rhythms and regularities are also brought into play. In this sense the listener finds his own meaning in the music.

Whether this explanation of the nature of musical composition and reception is at all true is not our immediate concern, what matters is that it should be seen that this is essential to understanding Lévi-Strauss' theory of myth. According to this, myth is just like music in this respect also. The myth has a double valency in that it combines culturally identified empirical categories such as the raw and the cooked, high and low, fire and water, and so on, in terms of purely formal, 'musical' relationships. To the comprehension of the former the receiver of the myth brings his pre-existing cultural knowledge (hence the need for the analyst to study the ethnography behind the myths being analysed) and in the latter, the abstract relations of these, he finds his own meaning in that his own mind (essentially a structuring, classifying, and ordering agency) reintegrates the multifarious given levels of formal organization of the myths into the hearer's own mental structures.

Myths thereby provide the mind of their hearers with a system of cultural categories ordered according to the unconscious rational activity of the mind, in which that mind finds satisfaction by the contemplation of its own properties. Myth, like music, is a structural mirror held up to the mind, and if we notice a common image both in the mirror and the subject mind contemplating it, then this can only be because both of these, the subject and its object image, belong to the same order of reality.

Myths find structural patterns in empirical experience because the mind, in the last analysis, is part of that empirical world also. In the mind the myth is a mirror of nature. In the myth nature is a mirror of the mind.

Quite what Lévi-Strauss means by 'mind' in this respect is clearly very important. We must postpone a discussion of this until later, but for the time being, and anticipating myself a little, let me say that for Lévi-Strauss this 'mind' is not some Hegelian 'Geist'. Lévi-Strauss is a materialist through and through – his 'mind' is more analogous to a computer than to a soul. Pursuing the computer analogy, one might say that essentially Lévi-Strauss sees the mind's activity in creating and hearing myths – or music, for that matter – as rather like what would happen if a computer were to be given a programme which made it print out all possible permutations of a series of arithmetical relationships. If we further imagine that the computer could read its own print-out and draw conclusions from it we can see that it would find the underlying pattern in its printed-out 'messages' corresponding to its own inner programmed 'code'.

Myth, for Lévi-Strauss, is abstract, but this abstraction is derived from the basic structural 'programming' of the mind – itself a natural object. When this programming is applied to nature an inevitable structural harmony and reciprocal mirroring results.

Looked at in this light, we can see that Lévi-Strauss' analysis of myth is exactly comparable to his analysis of totemism. Like totemism, myth is seen as reflecting two realities at once, a social reality in which it expresses relationships between various aspects of social life and of cultural codes in general, and a natural reality in that it reflects the principles of the basic functioning of the mind. In both myth and totemism nature, understood as the fundamental principle and pattern of the brain, structures culture in the mind of man. For man, as we have seen Lévi-Strauss repeating after Rousseau, is in essence a natural being.

The inter-play of nature and the mind, anthropology and primitive cultures, is well illustrated by the case of totemism. Durkheim's attempted explanation of this was, as we saw, an extension of a presumably arbitrary social structure on to nature. Hence the *social* was for Durkheim the final cause in the case of totemism. But for Lévi-Strauss, it is nature, and not society, which is its final and determining cause. This is true in two different, but related senses. First, nature is the cause because Lévi-Strauss reverses the

Durkheimian chain of causality and makes a natural structure impress itself on culture (i.e. the system of natural species on the society rather than *vice versa*). This is to say no more than that totemism could not have been created in a society unless natural species had first existed. Yet in a second sense nature is again the cause of totemism since these natural classifications are themselves the constructions of the mind, which in Lévi-Strauss' view is entirely a natural entity. As we have seen, he believes that the mind splits and opposes, mediates and resolves by use of a binary structural logic, analogous to that found by Jakobson in phonetics. Yet binary opposition is not totally arbitrary. It is not the gratuitous creation of the mind because the mind, being natural, obeys laws similar to those which determine the overall shape of things in general. Hence binary oppositions are not merely forced on to nature by the mind but actually exist in nature in the sense that reality is not an indistinguishable unity. Species really are different, and, for totemism, that is all that matters. In the last analysis, the mind creates species as it does totemism; but the mind does so naturally according to Lévi-Strauss, and the distinctions which it creates do really exist in nature. Hence nature, as final cause, underlies both.

The linguistic analogy

If we compare Lévi-Strauss' approach to kinship, totemism, and myth with the unsatisfactory analysis of totemic social structures offered in *Primitive Classification* and discussed in the preceding chapter, we can see that essentially what Lévi-Strauss has done is to find a way out of the explanatory *impasse* encountered by Durkheim by means of recourse to reductive explanations in terms of natural causes. Durkheim could not get beyond this *conscience collective* and located the ultimate basis of the social categories of totemism in states of collective emotion irreducible to rational examination'. Lévi-Strauss, on the other hand, can provide an explanation of the final origins of the structure of totemism. Like the final causes of kinship and myth, these lie in nature. In kinship these final natural causes lie in man's sexual nature, but in the cases of totemism and myth they lie rather in his intellectual nature, in the fact of his being a rational animal. This reason is largely unconscious, but it is reason all the same, just as Jakobson's phonetic oppositions remain systematic and rational even though we are unaware of them. Where Durkheim failed, Lévi-Strauss claims to have found a basis for the rational and critical examination of the ultimate structures of human culture.

The key to this undertaking is the proposition that such cultural phenomena as kinship, myth and totemism are analogous in their structure to language, and function as codes. We have already seen that this is basic to Lévi-Strauss' treatment of them. Kinship was analysed in terms of its being a system of communication of women between intermarrying groups of men. Totemism was shown to be a language which enabled one to conceptualize one's own social structure and the relationships of different groups within it. Just as phonetic patterns can be inverted in languages so we saw Lévi-Strauss arguing that the system of signification which we find in totemism can be inverted to produce what we know as caste. Finally, myth was treated as a system of signs in which nature was represented in the mind and the mind was represented in nature. Here the communicative function of the language in question was not that of exchanging women between groups of men, or that of representing a society to its members, but rather that of enabling the mind to communicate with the outside world and the outside world with the mind.

In each one of these cases the communication system used arbitrarily defined signs. The definition of these signs was Durkheimian in that in each case it was conventional. In the case of kinship women remain the 'signs' of the system by the dictates of nature it is true, but even here the exact definition of the sign was determined by arbitrary conventions governing the application of kinship terms, the rule of incest avoidance etc. In the case of totemism the signs were conventionally defined groups of persons linked arbitrarily with animals or plant species, and in that of myth pieces of anecdotes whose connection with reality were determined entirely by cultural considerations. But Lévi-Strauss' analysis of these systems of communication owed much to Mauss, whose notion of reciprocity plays such a prominent part in the former's work on kinship and whose concentration on the implicit logic of systems like gift-giving provides the point of departure for Lévi-Strauss' structural interpretations.

C

But for the final explanations of these cultural codes Lévi-Strauss resorts to conclusions comparable to those of Jakobson in phonetics. These were that the basis of language is first of all a set of purely physiological constraints (those of the anatomy and physiology of the mouth and larynx), and secondly a set of mental principles which enabled speakers to encode and decode the physiologically produced sounds effectively (binary opposition). In the case of kinship the physical constraints are for Lévi-Strauss the biology of reproduction and the mental principles of the oppositions underlying reciprocity and exchange. As far as totemic systems are concerned, the external constraints are the nature of social groups and the distribution of plant and animal species. The inner, psychological constraints are those of a basic structural logic analogous to that found by Jakobson in phonetics, and the same applies to the case of myth. All languages reduce irrespective of their content or function to two basic realities – the external world of nature (which includes man's physiological and anatomical attributes), and the internal world of the mind. These two natural worlds, seen in intimate communication in the phenomenon of myth, are both open to scientific scrutiny and hold out hope for Lévi-Strauss of an explanatory conclusion different from that of Durkheim in *Primitive Classification*. For the further elaboration of the significance of this reductionism we must wait until later, but for the time being let us conclude that it could not exist in Lévi-Strauss' structuralism without the all important linguistic analogy.

3 Lévi-Strauss and Marx

In the first chapter of this book I looked at the main figures who stand behind Lévi-Strauss in the French tradition of sociology. In the second I shifted my attention to Lévi-Strauss himself and briefly examined his writings in three key areas. In the course of doing this I tried to show that Lévi-Strauss, in dealing with the problem of kinship systems in *Elementary Structures of Kinship*, or that of totemism in *The Savage Mind*, was in effect working out on the theoretical level solutions to problems of explanation inherent in Durkheim's sociocentric method. I showed what relevance the linguistic analogy and Lévi-Strauss' borrowings from structural linguists like de Saussure and Jakobson had for this undertaking and, at the end of the last chapter, I pointed out that Lévi-Strauss' resolution of the explanatory problems of kinship, myth, and totemism had led him to reduce all such cultural languages to two natural realities – the brain and the phenomenal world.

But the great figures of the French tradition are not the only ones on whom Lévi-Strauss has had cause to draw. Marx is also of great relevance to any attempt to understand Lévi-Strauss' theoretical approach, and it is to the question of Lévi-Strauss' use of Marx that I now want to turn. In doing so we shall see that a third problem associated with Durkheim's sociocentric method – that of the explanation of social change – also exists and that Lévi-Strauss incorporates Marx into his sociology largely as a means of resolving it. We shall also see that the two final explanatory realities of Lévi-Strauss' structuralism, the brain and the natural world, show up again in this context, except that now, transmuted into Marxist terminology, they correspond to ideology on the one hand and to the materialistic dialectic on the other.

Code and Message

One of Durkheim's major problems, and one stemming directly from the sort of sociocentric explanation which we have seen him using in *Primitive Classification* and elsewhere was that of coping with social change. The system of collective representations once identified with the collective conscience which supported it tended to take on a monolithic, unchangeable quality because individual parts of the consciousness could not influence it. De Saussure introduced a distinction between *langue* and *parôle* to which I have already briefly alluded and which contains an implicit solution to this problem. It is clear that in languages there must be a stable system of collective representations which determines the grammar, phonetics, semantics etc – otherwise no shared language could exist and consequently no communication. But it is clear that languages change. De Saussure's problem, in other words, is like that of Durkheim – the need to stress consensus, but also to account for change. His solution is to make a distinction between a collective, systematic structure on the one hand – the *langue* – and an individual, articulated speech, or *parôle*, on the other. Modern structuralists like Jacobson have re-named these Code and Message, and this may be a better terminology. Essentially, the idea is that no communication can occur without an already existing systematized, collectively understandable Code, but also that the sending of Messages by individuals will in the long run modify and restructure the Code. Hence if a particular set of signs are not used in some new circumstances they may be dropped altogether, while other signs may be brought in for new needs, old ones redefined, and so on. Putting the matter in Durkheimian terms de Saussure would have said that *langue* was proper to the *conscience collective*, but that the *parôle* of individual consciousness had a slow-acting effect on it by means of which the *langue* could be changed, even quite radically.

Another way of referring to the same sort of thing is to distinguish between *synchronic* and *diachronic* aspects of language. The synchronic is the dimension of language proper to *langue,* or Code as Jacobson calls it. It is the dimension at right angles to the temporal, the dimension of the instantaneous, atemporal and unchanging, the systematic, holistic and functional. The diachronic is the temporal dimension, the dimension of the succession of moments, of the passage of time, of change, evolution, decay and re-growth. In the synchronic time does not pass and information does not degrade. All processes are reversible. In the diachronic, entropy – or disorder – does tend to increase, processes cannot usually be reversed, and there is a directional element present which is lacking in the synchronic. The Code is the language as it exists in the synchronic, the Message as it exists in the diachronic. In morse code, for instance, the code-book, which is set out in two dimensional diagrammatic and systematic fashion, exists in the synchronic. The actual messages as they are tapped out as an irreversible succession of signs exist in the diachronic.

An example of the use of this idea can be found in Jakobson's approach to the study of aphasia.

According to Jakobson, there are two main forms of aphasia, or pathological loss of the capacity to speak. These he terms 'similarity disorder' and 'contiguity disorder'. In the case of similarity disorder, the aphasic cannot substitute the Code for the Message, the synchronic for the diachronic, and hence loses the ability to express similarity and stresses instead contiguity. This is manifested in an inability to deal with tautologies. For example, the aphasic can use the word 'bachelor' in association with 'flat', but cannot say a 'bachelor is an unmarried man'. Bachelor/unmarried man is an aspect of language as a synchronic Code. 'Bachelor-flat' is a diachronic stringing-together of two otherwise unassociated parts of the semantic code. Again, this type of aphasic finds it difficult to repeat words when asked to do so. 'Say "No".' 'No, I can't say it.' Similarly, he will be unable to find synonyms for words he is given, or be able to translate them into foreign languages even if he knows the language in question very well. This disorder applies as much to the ideas and the things which words represent as to the words themselves. Hence context is stressed and ideas will be grouped on some basis of contiguity rather than similarity. For example, a woman at the zoo could list animals in the order of seeing them but not into zoological groups. Metaphors escape this type of aphasic altogether, but metonymy is used a lot. Hence when asked to say 'window' the aphasic suffering from similarity disorder will say 'glass', when asked to repeat 'heaven' say 'God', and so on.

Contiguity disorder is, not unexpectedly, the exact contrary of this. Syntax – a contiguity feature in that it links words together – is lost altogether and what Jakobson calls 'word heaps', or telegraphic style results. Words endowed with purely grammatical function such as prepositions and articles go first, followed by everything else until only key words remain – the very key words which in similarity disorder disappear first. Metaphoric words are heavily used as substitutes once context is lost. Words like 'café' cannot be recognized or repeated if the linear order of the word is reversed ('féca'); that is, if a transposition is affected in the diachronic dimension.

In the case of these aphasics the disorder affecting either the synchronic or the diachronic aspects of language as the case may be is seen to affect the total system of linguistic phenomena, and as a result the processes of thought itself. It is as if persons suffering from these aphasias had developed personal ways of thought, or a 'thought-culture' which was peculiar to the type of aphasia from which they suffered. It is obvious that if Lévi-Strauss assumes that collective aspects of social life – real 'culture' – can be traced, in part at least, to common psychological propensities in men, then such individual manifestations of linguistic disorder may not be without their value in indicating two important aspects of the way in which systems of linguistic communications work. These two aspects are the synchronic and diachronic, the Code and the Message.

Seen in Durkheimian terms, culture is clearly Code. Durkheim represents it as the *conscience collective*, that is, as a complete synchronic system of collective representations. In what he has had to say about totemism and kinship we have seen Lévi-Strauss talking about these phenomena in terms of their being pseudo-linguistic systems whose main aim was to facilitate communication – that is, as codes. The whole point of his analysis of kinship for example is to try to show that all known kinship systems – understood as systems – are based on a common communicative code which designates some groups as wife-givers, some as wife-receivers, and which is, as we have seen, purportedly based on sister-exchange, itself the result of incest-avoidance. The Kariera four-part marriage-class system is a code in the sense that it is a synchronic, systematic and functional entity which allows communication, that is, exchanges of sisters, to take place between intermarrying groups of men. Similarly, totemism is a code which enables a system of natural nomenclature to function as the basis of social communications regarding the identity of individuals and that of groups.

The notion of the arbitrary nature of the linguistic sign is clearly very close to Lévi-Strauss' definition of culture in that it sees the latter as the non-natural, as the conventional, contingent and arbitrary, and we have already seen in the preceding chapter the uses to which Lévi-Strauss put this idea and the way in which he had recourse to it to get out of the Durkheimian tautologies regarding the explanation of the 'social'. In the case of the synchronic/diachronic and Code/Message distinctions we shall see that Lévi-Strauss uses this in an analogous way to resolve the remaining difficulty – that of the explanation of social change.

To consider totemism and kinship as codes as we have seen Lévi-Strauss doing above may not seem much of an improvement on Durkheim, but taken into account with the other side of the distinction – that of Message – the whole idea becomes very much more applicable to the problem of change.

Lévi-Strauss makes use of this distinction between Code and Message in the following way. The synchronic Code, since it is atemporal in the sense of being a dimension at right angles to the diachronic, is clearly something to which the notion of change does not apply. This is not because such codes do not change; it is rather that, as codes, their essence lies in a systematic relationship between the parts, and on consensus among the users regarding its structure. Change in this respect means disorganization of the system and a temporary loss of consensus. On the other hand, the Message, because it exists only in time and in the communication of one sign after another in a linear manner, obviously associates itself quite easily with the phenomenon of variation. The Message and the diachronic are what de Saussure referred to as *parôle*, and as I pointed out above, the problem of change in linguistic systems was encountered early on, and in such an obvious way that notions like *parôle* had to be introduced into linguistics in order to take account of it. Hence *langue* or Code exists as what Durkheim would have called collective representations, but *parôle* and Message constitute the use of the Code in such a way that it is constantly being built up in new ways by the exigencies of expression. Code underlies Message in that the latter relies on the former for communication to be possible at all. But equally, Message underlies Code in that the Code is constituted by the messages which make up actual communications.

Kinship and totemism, seen in the way in which we have looked at them above, are both obviously codes. They are analysed by Lévi-Strauss without regard to time, change or social evolution. He represents them as synchronic, finalized and complete systems – just like a language considered from the synchronic point of view. Actual societies however, like actual languages, exist in the diachronic. They undergo change, some very slowly, others very much more quickly. Seen in this context, the cultural codes become messages. They become the behaviour of real people in real-life situations. Lévi-Strauss' structuralist approach is perfectly appropriate to the study of culture as Code, but for the analysis of culture as Message it is elsewhere that we must turn.

The Marxism of Claude Lévi-Strauss

'I do not at all mean to suggest', says Lévi-Strauss, 'that ideological transformations give rise to social ones. Only the reverse is in fact true.'[1] Lévi-Strauss' structuralism clearly does not lead to neo-Comteanism, assuming for a moment the rather too simple interpretation of the Law of the Three Stages which makes it appear that intellectual evolution causes social evolution. What Lévi-Strauss is effectively saying here is that he regards himself as a Marxist, as well as a structuralist, and says that it is to 'the theory of superstructures, scarcely touched on by Marx' that he wishes to make his contribution.[2] Cultural codes such as kinship and totemism are therefore apparently seen as ideologies, as theoretical constructions which justify, rationalize and explain reality rather underlie it. It is to Marxism that we must look if we want to find the *causes* of the phenomena which Lévi-Strauss considers.

A substratum of Marxist sentiment would not, of course, be surprising in Lévi-Strauss if we take into account the political and intellectual background of most contemporary French intellectuals. In the course of the Second World War, to go back no further than that, Marxism was associated with the Resistance movement, and with the liberation of France it enjoyed a respectability and popularity among intellectuals and *literateurs* which was only partly compromised by the development of the Cold War. Sartre, as we shall see later, as major luminary of existentialism, the fashionable intellectual movement which immediately preceded the rise of structuralism, saw it necessary to attempt a synthesis of existentialism, phenomenology and Marxism. Actually, Lévi-Strauss' Marxism is also clearly related to phenomenological influences, and it is as well to note that *The Savage Mind*, the book in which he discusses his position with regard to Marxism most clearly, is dedicated to the memory of Maurice Merleau-Ponty, who was an acknowledged major influence on Sartre as well as on Lévi-Strauss and numerous others of their generation.

But it would be quite wrong to dismiss Lévi-Strauss' claims to some sort of Marxist orthodoxy, such as those which I have quoted from *The Savage Mind*, as mere fashionable intellectual window-dressing. His Marxism goes much deeper than this and is, as we shall now see, an integral part of his sociological approach with regard to the problem of change.

We may sum up the argument of the previous section by saying that, in Marxist terms, Code is superstructure. What this means is that the underlying social cause of cultural systems such as totemism and Australian kinship systems is the dialectic. This dialectic, which is materialist of course, is itself dependent on the relations of the individuals of the society in question to the means of production at their disposal. Hence it is material causes which determine cultural codes, and cultural codes which rationalize, justify, and sustain the causative influences of material conditions.

Let us take totemism as an example of this. Lévi-Strauss denies that this is 'the outcome of a conceptual game taking place in the mind'.[3] Instead, he maintains that totemism should be seen as an ideology which is purely superstructural to a social system whose infrastructure is a set of material relations of production. Hence the choice of totemism as a social structure is not fortuitous. Its causes are to be found in its relation to the means of production in aboriginal society – means of production which are, presumably, at such a low level of technological development that private property does not exist. Hence the relationship between man and nature obtrudes to such an extent that in totemism nature is made an ideological system for comprehending culture.

In the case of traditional Indian society, the greater development of the means of production makes the caste system possible, and this can clearly be seen as an 'ideology' in the sense that notions about ritual pollution, caste commensality and occupational specialization obviously can be seen to function to justify and rationalize a certain system of production. Here the mind, understood as the creator of ideology in its structural aspects, is seen as operating on principles strictly comparable to those utilized in the creation of totemism, but as in the case of the aborigines, it is the dialectic of material relations which determines the social structure in terms of real social relationships.

The rôle of cultural codes like totemism and caste is merely one of structuring and making intelligible the given social relations. The Message in the case of these examples is the social action, the actual working out of the system on the ground and in real relations between people and things. An actual marriage is a message to the code of kinship, a ritual gathering is the diachronic expression of totemism as opposed to the synchronic totemic ideology. As in the comparable situation regarding language, it is the sending of messages, *parôle*, social action, which in fact alters and reconstitutes the codes, albeit very gradually in most cases.

In the final volume of his *Mythologiques* Lévi-Strauss remarks that the Second Law of Thermodynamics does not apply to the world of myths.[4] As we shall see in the last chapter, what goes for myths goes also for totemism, and kinship, not to mention cooking, table manners, and a thousand other things. This remark interestingly eludicates what Lévi-Strauss considers the relation between Code and Message to be, in the sense in which I have been using these terms. The Second Law, in its simplest form, states that entrophy increases with time, and applies equally well to the theory of information as to classical thermodynamics. Entropy, in terms of information theory, means 'noise' or disorganization as opposed to information and organization. In actual use – that is, as Message – codes become degraded in that irreversible (diachronic) changes occur which tend, on the whole, towards increasing entrophy, or disorder. A Kariera-type kinship system, for example, will, because of demographic difficulties not to mention the disturbing influence of human passions, tend to become distorted in time in that irregular marriage choices may occur or particular marriage-classes may grow very large while others dwindle. These sorts of changes result from the fact that culture as Message exists in an irreversible, diachronic flux of time and in a world of realities – realities which, on the whole, obey the Second Law. But as Code, culture exists in a fully reversible, non-degradable environment in which repair and reorganization of the system is always going on. This repairing and restructuring process is, in cybernetic terms, the exact equivalent to Marx's ideological processes – typically those of rationalization, justification and idealization. Marx interprets ideology in a disparaging way, seeing it broadly as a perversion of the truth – truth of course lying in the networks of material relations to the means of production. Lévi-Strauss sees it as this too, but he also ascribes a non-tendentious (one might almost say, non-ideological) function to ideology, in maintaining the intelligibility of codes, making this the structural and synchronic equivalent of Marx's diachronic and dialectical use of the term. This is the Durkheimian side of Lévi-Strauss' approach – the theoretical approach to culture which sees it as a system of collective representations, whereas in talking about determinants of change Lévi-Strauss is using an essentially Marxist approach, that of reducing culture to the materialist dialectic.

Summing up the situation then, one might say that strictly speaking Lévi-Strauss has *two* sociological methods, not one. To the analysis of culture as Code he brings Durkheimian structural positivism – a theoretical approach which, as we have seen, emphasizes functional integrity, holism, and normative consensus, but which is poorly endowed to cope with problem of change. To the analysis of culture as Message Lévi-Strauss brings a more or less conventional Marxism which sees society as the outcome of conflicting material relations and is well equipped to deal with the issue of social change. The structuralist approach relates only to superstructures which, as we have seen, can themselves ultimately be reduced to a materialistic basis in brain physiology – a point to which we shall have to return again later. The Marxist approach, by contrast, applies only to infra-structure and although providing reductive explanations of social change, cannot address itself to the quite different question of the explanation of the structuring processes of ideological superstructures as such.

Thus just as de Saussure in his classic work on linguistics distinguished two linguistic sciences – linguistics of *langue* (Code), and linguistics of *parôle* (Message) – so Lévi-Strauss is implicitly assuming two quite different sociological methods – Durkheimian positivism modified to become Straussian structuralism, and Marxist dialectics seen as a means of explaining social change, conflict and the final social causes of cultural codes. These two types of explanatory approaches correspond to the dual form of his materialist reductionism to the workings of the mind in a social context (positivistic structuralism) and to the external world of material causes (Marxist dialectics). Put in its simplest form, we can sum up by saying that Lévi-Strauss' structuralism, derived as it is from Durkheim, Mauss and de Saussure, applies to the synchronic dimension of social phenomena, and that his Marxism applies accordingly to the diachronic perspective.

Durkheim and Marx

Reverting in conclusion to my example from Jakobson on the subject of aphasia, we might say that, seen against the background of the pathology of aphasia which Jakobson has suggested, Durkheim would appear to be a sociologist with, theoretically speaking, something of a contiguity disorder, and Marx would appear as one with a corresponding similarity disorder, if by the latter we mean an inability or disinclination to deal with the synchronic dimension of social life. Durkheim, as we have seen, deals exclusively with the synchronic wholes which make up social codes – the *conscience collective* – and pathologically, form the point of view of sociological theory, ignores the continuity or diachronic and historical dimension. Marx, on the other hand, with his exclusive preoccupation with social change, runs the risk of losing altogether the 'key words', or ideologies of social life by stressing only the dialectic.

Metonymy, the characteristic style of similarity disorder aphasics, manifests itself in Marx as an obsessional tendency to reduce all phenomena to their associated material aspects – the (metonymic) relations to the means of production. The statement to the effect that all history is the history of class conflict is clearly metonymic in this sense. Durkheim, on the other hand, employs metaphors, the typical pathology of contiguity disorder aphasics, ultimately to the extent of seeing the *conscience collective* as a socio-metaphysical equivalent of God, as I suggested earlier. Indeed, the whole organismic analogy underlying sociocentrism in all its forms is the metaphorical equivalent of the equally one-sided and unsatisfactory Marxist metonymic equation of history with class conflict. Syntax, or in theoretical sociological terms, dialectics, disappears altogether in Durkheim leaving only the 'key words' – the collective representations. In the case of dialectical materialism it is these key collective representations 'largely untouched by Marx' which constitute the main shortcomings in Lévi-Strauss' eyes. Rather like a Russian novelist mentioned by Jakobson who suffered from similarity disorder and tended to metonymy and the splitting of his characters into two halves whilst writing in a highly naturalistic style, Marx appears to have split society metonymically into two classes and to have stressed a different but analogous sort of naturalism, that of nineteenth-century materialism.

Lévi-Strauss' theoretical relation to Marx and Durkheim is analogous to that of a normal speaker to aphasics. He implicitly suffers from both disorders while manifesting neither because, of course, a use of both similarity and contiguity, synchronic and dia-chronic, Code and Message, is essential for the expression of normal linguistic thought. In a sociological sense then, Lévi-Strauss represents a synthesis of these two, one-sided and perhaps pathological tendencies in sociological theory.

He is not a Marxist in the conventional meaning of the term, but he does appear to feel, like many of his generation, that an intellectual genuflection before the altar of dialectical materialism is an essential requirement for ideological respectability. In the case of his theoretical sociology this ideological conformity to convention means the apparent ability to explain social change while still holding on to the most valuable parts of the Durkheimian system. But quite apart from the usefulness of Marx as a corrective to Durkheim's too static sociocentrism, the sociology of Marx has another rôle to play in Lévi-Strauss' structuralism, and it is to a consideration of this that we must now turn. As we shall see, this is in the context of the traditional sociological concern with the rôle of values in social science.

4 The debate with Sartre

I alleged at the beginning of this book that Lévi-Strauss belongs among the great scholastics of sociological thought and that theoretically speaking his position is not so very far away from sociologists like Talcott Parsons or Merton. I characterized the scholastic sociologist as a worker of synthesis between rival sociological schools and as a compendium-maker of the theories of great classical writers such as Durkheim, Marx or Weber. In the last chapter, I argued that, from the theoretical point of view, Lévi-Strauss' structuralism can indeed be seen to be a synthesis, or at least a mixing, of Durkheim and Marx, and we have seen that ideas from a whole host of other writers such as de Saussure, Jakobson, Mauss and even Comte are also included in Lévi-Strauss' system.

This fusion of Marxist dialectics and Durkheimian positivism of course raises its own problems, and in particular it raises the traditional one regarding the correct place of values in sociological research. This is because Durkheimian positivism appears to rule out value judgements whereas Marxism appears to demand them. Nowhere is Lévi-Strauss' resolution of this problem better seen than in his debate with Sartre. But Sartre is himself something of a scholastic in sociology, and before going on to the debate itself I would like to draw my readers' attention to the extent to which Sartre represents a trend in sociological thought closely comparable to that found in the works of Talcott Parsons. Such an exercise will also go some way to illustrating the relevance of Sartre's writings to those of Lévi-Strauss.

Sartre and Talcott Parsons

Talcott Parsons begins his *Structure of Social Action* by considering the major traditions in sociological thought up to his time. These he lists as the utilitarian approach of classical economics, the positivist approach of Comte and his successors, and the German Idealist school. Having reviewed the strengths and weaknesses of each, Talcott Parsons goes on to show how all three can be synthesized into a single theory which has the strengths of all but the weaknesses of none – the Parsonian Voluntaristic Action Theory. He then goes on to consider the simplest possible social situation, a sociological microsm in which only two persons are represented – *Ego* and *Alter*. Their mutual interaction is shown to produce reciprocal expectations which lead to rôle-playing *vis à vis* one another, the development of shared behavioural norms etc. These microcosmic, dyadic relationships are then seen as built up into social groups and institutions, and finally into the whole society.

Jean-Paul Sartre's approach in his *Critique de la raison dialectique* is strikingly similar, despite the vast differences in background and sociological tradition which exist between the two men. He too begins by reviewing what he claims to be the two major philosophies of modern times – Marxism and Existentialism – and goes on to suggest that a synthesis of the two naturally leads to a new theory of society which is, initially at least, strongly reminiscent of that of Talcott Parsons.

Sartre, too, begins with a social microcosm of two persons – the Each and the Other. The Each perceives the Other, and *vice versa*, and in doing so each begins to see the other as a limitation to his existential freedom of choice. Each begins to *objectify* the other, to deny the other's inalienable existential freedom to create his own essence out of his own existence by postulating a false essence for the other as anterior to his existence – a process distinctly analogous to Parsons' rôle-playing. Again like Parsons, Sartre proceeds to build up a system of reciprocating expectations which he sees as constituting, via a series of intermediate steps called the Series, Group-in-Fusion etc, social institutions and eventually society itself. Here the jargon is French, Marxist and Existentialist rather than Teutonic-American, Functionalist and sociological, but beneath the terminology fundamental similarities between Sartre and Talcott Parsons remain.

However, a key difference between Sartre and Parsons, and one which in fact brings out the similarity between the former and Lévi-Strauss enters in very early on when Sartre begins to speak of scarcity as a phenomenon underlying objectification and proceeds to build this into his existentialist sociology as a major means of reconciling it with Marxism whose holistic, historical and materialistic bias he sees corrected by the individualistic, psychological and phenomenological nature of existentialism. The result being an all-embracing philosophy of social and individual existence. In making Marxism an essential part of his sociological theory, Sartre is clearly doing something comparable to what we have seen Lévi-Strauss attempting in making up for the deficiencies of Durkheimianism when faced with the problem of social change. But the difference between them is that where Sartre has grafted on to Marxism an individualistic philosophy of subjective awareness, Lévi-Strauss has instead maintained a Durkheimian position on the issue of the possibility of an objective science of social facts and consequently has seen fit to merge Marxism with positivism by means of the modified Durkheimian approach which we have seen to be the basis of his structuralism. The social-psychological aspects of Sartre's existentialist-Marxism however are in fact much closer to the unmodified Durkheimian position than would appear on the surface, but a detailed consideration of this would take us too far from our subject. Suffice it to say that the hidden Durkheimianism of Sartre's social psychology is another point of comparison with the sociology of Talcott Parsons and of them both with Lévi-Strauss.

Structural positivism

This similarity in aim between the sociologies of Sartre and Lévi-Strauss, namely that of wanting to make up for what is lacking in Marx, leads directly to the central issue of the debate, which is, quite simply, about the exact nature of what is needed. For Sartre, as we have seen, what is needed is Existentialism, but for Lévi-Strauss the added ingredient is that which is required for the understanding of the synchronic, structural dimension of social life – the structural positivism derived from Durkheim and Mauss, de Saussure and Jakobson.

If we neglect for a moment a number of minor details such as their respective conceptions of what anthropology is or should be, I think that one can see that a great deal of what Sartre says in his

Critique de raison dialectique is entirely compatible with Lévi-Strauss' position. The real difference and issue of contention is that Lévi-Strauss wishes to secure a domain for positive, scientific knowledge about man – structural anthropology, linguistics etc, – and Sartre, for his part, wishes to see all reason as dialectical, and all knowledge as contributing to reconstitute rather than to dissolve man. To put it more simply, Sartre wants to see anthropology adding fuel to the ideological fires of Marxism in its struggle against atrophying, academic, static, Analytical Reason, and sees Lévi-Strauss' positivism as compromising this position. Since for Sartre reason is a function of the movement of the dialectic, it is clear that reason, if it is to be a true partner in it, must be equally dialectical, and that the dialectic of Reason, like that of materialism, must be one permanently moving forward by antithetical progressions and finding its only final truth in its relation to the end of the whole process – the resolution of contradictions originating in the first place in the phenomena of scarcity. Since this final resolution cannot be achieved until the classless society comes into being it follows that neither the present state of materialist dialectic, nor that of Dialectical Reason can be judged definitive, but must rather be seen as temporary and contingent, a mere stage on the way. Thus for Sartre true knowledge is dialectical knowledge which is relative knowledge. In such a situation positive, analytical and absolute knowledge cannot be other than a sham. It will inevitably arouse suspicions of being conservative and obscurantist, since, not being willing to move with the dialectic, it will be suspected of moving against it.

What Lévi-Strauss is effectively saying in answer to this is that Sartre is mistaken about the situation and that whilst his positivism in so far as it studies superstructure is outside the scope of Sartre's 'Dialectical Reason' then his view of what should constitute historical and non-structural sociological studies most definitely is not. Lévi-Strauss' concept of the latter is entirely dialectical for he sees historical knowledge reconstituted rather as the *bricoleur* reconstitutes new structures out of old – the means of reconstitution being historical elements, the end being the Revolution.

Lévi-Strauss goes to some lengths to show that certain historical theories, such as that concerning the *Fronde*[1] for example, may become *dépassé* in Sartre's sense – may become overtaken by newer, more relevant re-constitutions of our historical knowledge – and that these re-constitutions may themselves, in the dialectical process become superseded by other, future historical perspectives.

Yet despite this, I think it will have struck the reader that there is apparently a profound discontinuity in Lévi-Strauss' method. The positivism he advocates, and applies to the study of structure, will not apparently do for the study of history, for if it did Sartre's criticisms would be entirely justified, and for the moving, dialectical process of historical ideology Lévi-Strauss would be attempting to substitute the fixed, dogmatic, academic conservatism of scientific knowledge. He would, in the eyes of Sartre the existentialist philosopher and Marxist, be de-humanizing man and treating the phenomenon of man as if it were a part of the non-human. For Sartre man is essentially a creature living in a state of permanent existential dilemma beset by a perpetual problem of choice. Such must inevitably mark him off absolutely from the domain even of other animate beings and consign him to the lonely state of privilege which is that of being the only free agent in an unfree and inhuman world. However, it is clear I hope that Lévi-Strauss is not doing this, and furthermore could not do so, for this would result in a confusion between the two opposed dimensions, synchronic/ diachronic, structure/history, Code/Message. All that Lévi-Strauss in his Structural Positivism is claiming is that the principles and structures of the codes remain the same but that the message varies. Thus Sartre has no need to fear that Lévi-Strauss is condemning Marxism to a fixed immutable message; he is not. He is merely say-ing that structural positivism, if I may call it that, does not apply to it any more than the principles of structural linguistics in any way compromise individuals' freedom of linguistic expression from the point of view of what they say.

The uncertainty principle of the social sciences

Lévi-Strauss has encapsulated his doctrine on the explanatory competence of structural positivism in terms of what he has called the 'uncertainty principle' of the social sciences. This says nothing more than that our understanding of our own society, or of sociology, is quite distinct from the understanding we have of other, foreign societies isolated from our historical tradition. Lévi-

Strauss' point elaborated in *Tristes Tropiques* and other works is that we may either grasp the structure of a society and relinquish historical, empathic understanding of it as content, or we may become part of a society's history and thereby lose our chance of detached structural insight. Hence a structural anthropology of our own society is impossible because we are all far too much involved in the historical necessity of our own society to be able to achieve it. To put the matter in Marxist terms, one might say that since we all share in the ideologies of our own society we cannot merely by taking thought distract ourselves from them and see them as if we were 'pure visitors'. Our entire mode of thinking is allegedly so determined by our historical and social environment that such objectivity is not possible according to Lévi-Strauss. Such a position is, as we have seen, entirely in accordance with the traditional abhorrence felt by sociology for pure philosophy.

But with regard to other societies a truly objective type of knowledge is possible. In their case the opposite is true. In a primitive society it is almost impossible for one of us to achieve true empathic understanding – to become a part of the historical necessity of that society – for the simple reason that we have come from our own. On the other hand, being a pure visitor to this society one is privileged with structural insight, if not with understanding of its historical and dialectical essence. This we can never know without abandoning our Western rationalism which is the basis of our structural scientific understanding. Essentially what we are doing, Lévi-Strauss argues[2] is to translate the terms of a primitive society into those of our own, substituting structure for content and form for essence while simultaneously we convert the content of our own society – our philosophical rationalism, scientific method – into the form of the other – kinship studies etc expressed as forms of the society in question. A two-way interchange occurs whereby information flows, via the method of structural anthropology, from one society to another. The scientific objectivity of the process is guaranteed in Lévi-Strauss' eyes, by the fact that our 'content' (class consciousness, European historical experience etc) cannot, or rather, need not pass directly into our understanding of the other society because it may well lack such things as class consciousness and have no history relevant to our own. Our ideology can only bridge the gap by becoming purely a structural code, a mere array of signs which, like the signs in music, signify nothing intrinsic but only their own extrinsic relations. Hence mythological analysis comes to resemble musical composition in a very striking manner. Our ideology, its content otherwise irrelevant, becomes just as objective as it does in relation to the physical world, where class consciousness and historical involvement are just as superfluous. Positive scientific understanding of societies therefore assumes the form of a science of structural transformations mediating between our consciousness and that of other men in other societies. In this respect it is a department of communications science.

But as far as our own society is concerned the opposite is the case. Here there can be no objective structural study, for the application of our own theories to our own doings is bound to be more or less circular since final causes exist for Lévi-Strauss not in the conscious mind but in the Materialistic Dialectic. Having sided with Sartre and having denied the possibility of objective conscious knowledge independent of historical necessity Lévi-Strauss has denied for ever the possibility of the sort of certain, uncontrovertible social knowledge naïvely believed to reside in a natural science of society by St Simon and Comte. But in its place Lévi-Strauss has put a more subtle social knowledge and, following Marx, made it dependent on the dialectic of history. This does not deny the possibility of true historical and social knowledge of our own society, it merely maintains that all our knowledge is conditional on the historical process and that it is in history and not in the consciousness of individual minds that ultimate and final truth exists.

We live, according to Lévi-Strauss[3] in 'hot societies', that is, in societies driven by the energy of social differentiation. Truth, sociological truth, lies in understanding this. It is difficult in this case to pin down such Marxist doctrines to ultimate proofs. As sociologists are well aware, 'social reality', whatever that might be, is infinitely debatable and doubtless the only arguments that can be adduced to justify the Marxist position in the present case are those that reason from present conditions and attempt to show that the Marxist theory is the most plausible in accounting for the facts. But this in itself involves great difficulties since one might accept the theory but reject its import, believe that the proletarians would ultimately triumph but reject this conclusion as morally undesirable. Marxism resides ultimately on a sort of St Simonian moral assumption which, whilst doubtless defended by Marxists as self-evidently true, can nevertheless be rejected by non-believers, and does not in any case constitute real positive truth. Ethics is notoriously controversial. The other alternative is to reject the ethical doctrine as 'philosophical' and consequently impoverished and ideologically suspect, and instead rely entirely on the sociological doctrine of the inevitability of class conflict and of proletarian victory. But in this case, if ultimate proletarian victory is not postulated as morally the right end, then it can only have any compulsion if it is stated to be the historically, dialectically proper end. No other apologetic is possible if the class struggle is still in progress. If the Revolution is not seen as morally right it cannot be justified entirely on grounds of fact since this would involve a belief in its historical inevitability and this can only come by faith. Prior to the apocalypse circumstances are always ambiguous and historical evidence always controvertible. The Marxist apologist cannot put too much reliance on reason alone since, as I have already pointed out, this would, if taken too far, compromise the doctrine of the ideological nature of all thought and its dependence of the dialectic.

It is not my intention to embark on a long methodological critique of Marxism, or to explore fully the few remarks above. My point is only to try to show that Lévi-Strauss' Marxism relies on grounds of proof very different from those of his positive structural method. In the latter case the perennial scientific criteria of parsimony, comprehensiveness and theoretical elegance must remain the ultimate standards, to which may be added the demand for a notional materialistic reductionism since we must not forget that this is a form of positivism which, like the Marxist variety, is prejudiced against pure philosophy and requires a tangible empiricism at its base. In the former case, that of historical, Marxist positivism, Lévi-Strauss' position is that historiography, statistics, archaeology, demography and other studies can all contribute scientific truths to modern sociology. But ultimately, sociology, if it is to take account of the past, must realize that historical knowledge is dependent on present conditions, is given to change. This does not mean that such changing historical theories are in any way false. It is merely the result of the fact, amply obvious, that the present is the outcome of the past and that those factors shaping the present and consequently also our picture of the past are themselves an outcome of the past by the dialectical process. History in this case is, as I remarked before, the ultimate finality. Until history is completed, final explanation, of necessity, must remain incomplete. The provisional, incomplete nature of historical knowledge results from this fact. In the case of structural positivism, however, it is first and foremost the collective, rational unconscious, itself dependent on brain physiology, which is the final cause. Since this finality is always with us and is not subject to the revelation of history through time it is consequently, in principle at least, knowable in a complete sense, in just as complete a sense as the world of inanimate nature.

It is clear I think that, as I have been arguing all along, Lévi-Strauss is distinguishing two final causes, both the mind and the dialectic, and attributing to each a different form of positivism. In the case of history the relevant final cause is the dialectic of material relations and the appropriate science what I have termed Marxist positivism. This treats of our social expression in a diachronic, irreversible time dimension analogous to what de Saussure called *parôle*. This is a more indefinite, progressive, continually growing and developing reality, one which in Sartre's terminology constantly 'de-totalizes' and 're-totalizes', that is, continually dissolves and yet re-constitutes the system. It is an articulation of content, an expression of subjective meaning, it is history as the 'speech' of society. Opposed to this is the synchronic, reversible time dimension of what we might term structure. Here the final causes lie within the mind itself and ultimately within the mind as a physical and natural object, as was pointed out above. Here the appropriate science is structural, Durkheimian positivism. This considers our social expression as *langue*, or Code – as a mechanism arrested in its movement, as a closed and complete system of relations. It is the means by which we express, it is the objective structure of expression. Ultimately it is the form in which the mind casts the content which history and the dialectic prescribe for it.

The 'uncertainty principle' declares the necessity to distinguish these two quite different dimensions of sociological analysis, and the reason for this can easily be seen. To confuse the science of social life considered as a code with that of society in the process of expression would be to return to earlier forms of positivism where it was thought that a positive understanding of society in the present inevitability guaranteed the same sort of understanding of it in the past and future. In Lévi-Strauss' eyes this would be like confusing Caesar's latin grammar with his interpretation of the events of the Gallic Wars. In this case grammar appertains to an element of language considered as a code; the actual sense of the book, the sequence of ideas expressed by virtue of the grammar to the Message. To fail to recognize the crucial distinction between code and message, structure and content, will either result in an idea of society as a shifting, changing and unstructured chaos – a thermodynamic flux one might call it, or on the other hand, and going to the opposite extreme, it will result in its conception as a fixed, unchanging system mechanically repeating a limited repertoire of activities. The latter is the extreme to which most Durkheimian positivists tend – in other words, towards a mechanistic sociology in which social change is problematic or epiphenomenal. The former alternative tends to be the equally unrealistic outcome of stress on change and dialectics found in the works of writers like Sartre.

History as a code

We are now in a position to understand fully the Sartre/Lévi-Strauss controversy. Essentially the problem is that Sartre, insisting that all knowledge should be dialectical, progressing, changing and self-transcending, appears to be denying the very possibility of stable, systematic and 'analytical' knowledge. Lévi-Strauss is replying that whilst the former, dialectical form of knowledge is appropriate to the ever-progressing onward movement of man through time, through history, an analytical, formal and thoroughly systematic knowledge is possible in an opposed dimension of the instant in which the mind, ever subject to the dialectic as all good Marxists must believe it to be, constantly formulates its ideological vision in terms of fixed, recurrent and ultimately universal mental characteristics. These characteristics are the form of thought exhibited in all mythologies, indeed, in all codes whether linguistic, geneological, culinary or historical.

Looked at against the background of all that has been said so far it will become clear I think that historical discourse qualifies as such a code in every respect. For a code to exist there must be a system of signs, and signs, if they are not to be natural symbols limited in their power of reference must be arbitrary in the sense that they must be different in nature from the reality which they represent. If this is lacking then we are not talking of sign-systems and their characteristics. A car blocking my path is not a sign in this sense, but a red traffic-light does function as one and, since it is one, involves with it the whole question of a system of significant relationships which can function intelligibly to represent what should be represented but which for whatever reason cannot be immediately experienced. Hence traffic lights provide information on the movement of vehicles which could not be definitely known if the traffic-light system had not existed. When the light is green I know for certain that I can proceed and that the other traffic at the junction is stationary. Similarly with language, where I know the sense of what I want to say but, lacking powers of thought-transference, resort to words to signify my intention.

In this respect history functions as a code since like all codes, historical events are signs which are at least *a priori* arbitrary since, like all activities of the mind, history is ideological and determined by other, non-mental realities. Thus social statistics, archaeology and historiography must be taken to be exact analytical sciences according to Lévi-Strauss; but history itself, the articulation, the interpretation and the final expression of these exact sciences remains inevitably wedded to an arbitrary system of signs. This results from the fact that the final significance of the terms it uses derives from their relation to other terms and because history is itself handed down to us by tradition. As in the case of the phonetic structure 'apple', we use the sign not because there is some necessary *a priori* natural determinant (there cannot be, since some people say '*pomme*'), but because we happen to be English speakers. Similarly, 1789 is significant to the French not because 1789 is a universal fact of nature, like the fact that there are about 365 days in a year, but rather because they are French, living in the twentieth century, and we must assume, of liberal persuasions.[4]

In other words, we must see that historical expressions, like those of language, myth or totemism, select significant units from a pre-existing and distinct terminological matrix. In the case of language this is a series of sounds, in that of myth numerous other codes such as nature-lore and cooking, in that of totemism, natural classifications. In the case of history this matrix from which signs are selected is that of the series of historical events.

The necessity of history, and of all the paraphernalia of past events and chronologies that go with it, results from the sociological fact that we live in what Lévi-Strauss terms 'hot societies'. I have mentioned this before, and all the metaphor really means is that we live in societies in which the dialectic is constantly producing social change. Hence the need to express our ideological and contingent consciousness of this ceaseless change in terms which are themselves appropriate to such a situation because themselves drawn from a temporal and changing series, namely history itself.

History, like myth and music, has a double valency. Like music it refers itself to two realities at once. To a natural one, in the sense that historical messages, just like all human communications and especially like music refer finally to the natural form of the mind, to its inner invariable structure, which in both primitive kinship systems and in the sophistications of modern historical thought exhibits the same general characteristics. But like music, history relates also to a cultural formation in the mind, quite apart from its natural element. In the case of history this cultural structure goes far beyond anything found in any other code with the one exception of myth. Like myth, history is a code of codes, a structure of structures, like it it builds up all other aspects of culture into great conceptual constellations and yet, transcending culture, myth, and that aspect of myth which we call history, relates to the essential determination of culture, to the very root of social life, to the dialectic of material relations and to the final causes of society itself.

Culture is production in that culture is not given by nature but is extracted by man from what nature provides. Material production for the Marxist is the true ground of cultural activity and in the case of history – the social myths of 'hot societies' – these conditions of production constantly work to produce the progress of the dialectic and provide the impetus to its final resolution. Thus by contrast to the science of the structures of the mind, the science of this aspect of history demands something as yet uncompleted, something particular to our own past and founded on the true realization of

the potential of the dialectic. It demands a form of positive knowledge complementary to that of the synchronic and the structural, it
demands, in other words, Marxism itself.

Social science and social values

In conclusion, one can show that the whole discussion between
Lévi-Strauss and Sartre, and the principle of uncertainty which Lévi-
Strauss claims to have found as a fundamental ground-rule for the
social sciences, can be very easily understood in terms of the
traditional sociological controversy concerning the place of values
in sociological investigation.

We may sum up the 'uncertainty principle' in terms of Jakobson's
Code/Message distinction by saying that, as social analysts, we
cannot speak the message and know the code at one and the same
time. In our own societies our thinking is Message, with regard to
others it is Code. The moment we begin to think the Code we transform it into a message since thinking about our own society is a
diachronic and ideological process. The demand that anthropology
should be the structural study of the social codes of societies whose
dialectic escapes us is methodologically equivalent to a demand that
sociological investigations of primitive societies should be
positivistic. On the other hand, the statement that thinking about
our own society is Message implies the impossibility of abstract-
ing our understanding of it from our participation in it.

Lévi-Strauss' resolution of this uncertainty principle is in reality
nothing more than an implied solution to the traditional methodological issue surrounding the place of values in sociological research. Values are defined for the purposes of this debate as subjective and tendentious, and usually contrasted with facts, which are
imagined to be objective and neutral. Values always imply some
sort of commitment to choice, whether it be political, aesthetic or
whatever. In terms of the linguistic analogy and the Code/
Message distinction, the sending of a message always implies
a choice of elements of the code, whereas the code implies all possible choices and all possible messages. Sociological understanding
of our own society is a message in this sense in that it necessitates statements about particular economic, political and social
choices determined by the dialectic, whereas an understanding of

other societies is only in terms of structural possibilities of a total system of transformations. The latter is equivalent to Jakobson's study of phonetics – it lists structural possibilities of the phenomenon in question understood as Code – whereas the former is analogous to actually speaking one particular language and hence choosing one particular set of phonemes. Put very simply, what Lévi-Strauss is saying is that when we come to look at our own society we always are inclined to become committed, merely because it is our own society. But when we study other, primitive societies, we can manage to be much more detached and objective.

It is clear from my remarks above that the use of the Code/Message distinction, when identified with a Durkheimian-positivist/dialectical-materialist opposition, effectively comes to represent a dichotomy between objectivity on the one hand, and subjectivity on the other. The Code, the province of Durkheimianism and structural anthropology, is the equivalent of positivistic facts. The Message, the subjective articulation of cultural codes, is the equivalent of values and ideology. Structural anthropology can only study structure and Code because the values, the commitment to the ideological subjectivity of primitive societies is lacking in the anthropologist, almost by definition. Equally, structural anthropology is inapplicable to contemporary societies because, as social analysts looking into our own societies, we cannot help, and ideally must declare our values. Lévi-Strauss thus resolves the problem of the respective spheres of influence of facts and values with the further useful and desirable addition of declaring just what these values must be. Quite obviously, he finds them to be the ideology of Marxism, a commitment to which necessitates, as we have seen, the abandonment of a structural analysis of Western societies, but one which also brings in train with it the possibility of an objective and ideologically quite neutral study of societies alien to our own. Thus for Lévi-Strauss sociology cannot be limited to values alone, to a thorough-going subjectivism of the sort we expect from Phenomenology, but neither can it restrict itself to a positivistic study of social facts as Durkheim had believed. A judicious balancing of the two enables him to represent his own theory as something which sociologically is almost all things to all men.

5   Lévi-Strauss and Freud

At the beginning of this book I promised to set Lévi-Strauss in the context of sociology as a whole, and in order to do this I had to summarize briefly the relevant parts of the sociologies of Comte and Durkheim, Mauss, Marx and Sartre. I also undertook to give a detailed exegesis of his sociological method and in the course of doing this I showed how he had made use of structural linguistics and how his works contained material pertinent to the enduring problems of sociological research. But throughout I have only hinted at what is the most significant theoretical issue in all Lévi-Strauss' work, namely his reductionism; and I have avoided an examination of his works in the context of the person who has had greatest impact upon them, namely Freud. The time has now come to consider these final questions, and in the course of so doing to come to some conclusions about Lévi-Strauss' real significance and value to contemporary sociological thought.

The structuralist myth

Lévi-Strauss has remarked on more than one occasion that structural anthropology is a sort of myth. This is because, like history, it is a code whose purpose it is to resolve contradictions and to enable men to communicate with one another. So far we have been mainly concerned with just how Lévi-Strauss believes this structural code should be constituted. It is now necessary to ask ourselves what such a code could ultimately mean and what the final significance of Lévi-Strauss' sociology might be.

It is, as we have seen, an elaborate and ingeniously contrived system of sociological explanation which appears, on the surface at least, to have much to recommend it. Its eclecticism appears to be its greatest strength. Any sociological theory which can comprehend and contain so many conflicting tendencies appears to be worthy of close attention. Again, any theoretical approach which can lead to so many apparently new and important insights into kinship, myth, social structure and so on, not to mention cooking, tattooing, classifying and theorizing, clearly claims the serious attention of all students of the social sciences.

If we were to ask Lévi-Strauss to tell us, in terms of structuralism, what his structural anthropology might be we already know what the answer would be. We saw in the last chapter that structural anthropology is a code which when expressed as a message – an anthropological work like *The Savage Mind* or *Mythologiques* – conveys information from primitive to modern culture in such a way that the society in question sees its cultural codes become anthropological message, just as we, in the receiving society, see our cultural message become structural anthropological code. The coded information flows across the gap between civilized and savage, 'hot' and 'cold', Western and colonial and, like all communications discussed by structuralists, obeys the basic Saussurian principles. Its *signs* – in this case anthropological propositions – are arbitrary. The theories of totemism, primitive kinship, myth etc etc which anthropologists like Lévi-Strauss produce are understood on the basis of this analogy as arbitrary signs whose purpose is to signify a reality that would otherwise be unintelligible to us – that of the culture (the codes) of another society isolated from our own. As signs, such theories are arbitrary because they cannot convey the *content* – the subjective element – of the culture in question except by way of its *structure*. Since structure is entirely relational and, in the last analysis, abstract, any content can only arise for us out of the form – the kinship, mythological or social structures with which anthropology confronts us.

When the anthropologist comes to study totemism, he does so by constructing theories which are – like totemism itself – structural categories originated in the mind and addressed to the problem of resolving nature – in this case the nature of a social organization – into an intelligible form. The anthropologist is trying to classify and to 'understand' totemism in just the same way as the native in constructing totemism 'understands' and classifies both nature and his own society.

To put it another way, one might say that both structural anthropology and primitive cultures are attempting to create codes by means of which to communicate. The substance of the code is quite different in each case – in one it is nature, in the other a primitive culture – but both use systems of signs in order to convey something to someone. In the case of totemism this something is a form of social organization which conveys to its users information about their own society and about how they relate to it. In the case of modern Western structural anthropology the information conveyed is about an alien culture whose structure is otherwise unintelligible to us.

It is in the last analysis a question of the modern Western mind's communication with a culture which is itself the creation of a primitive mind and hence of the establishment of a true communication whereby information flows from primitive to civilized by virtue of a science which seeks to convey to the reality of the primitive sophisticated symbolism capable of representing it. Anthropology, which is a part of our own culture and therefore determined by the dialectic, can be seen to have a definite part to play in our societies as *content* – as knowledge *for*. But with regard to alien cultures it can be only *structural* – containing knowledge *of* – and, as such part of the subjectivity of our own society which communicates to us the objectivity of another.

The analysis of myth fulfils the same function. Here the arbitrary signs, the mythemes, are in fact nothing more than linguistic equivalents of the supreme arbitrary fact – culture – or, in Durkheim's terminology, the mythemes are collective representations which relate to the totality of collective representations, the *conscience collective*. Lévi-Strauss' aim and that of Durkheim are identical in that both are attempting to make the phenomena of primitive culture, whether they be totemism or myths or whatever, intelligible to us by showing the relationships between these phenomena and the rest of the society and social structure. In this respect Lévi-Strauss' structuralism means no more, and no less, than did Durkheim's sociocentrics of which, in a sense, it can be seen to be a species. As a system of arbitrary signs, myth relies on a social consensus or, if you like, on culture, to give it meaning. If Lévi-Strauss conceived of myth as a collection of psychological symbols as Freud and Jung did, then this social dimension might not be at all important. For Freud, as in a different sense for Jung, symbols mean what they do by reference to the individual unconscious, even if in the case of Jung this individual unconscious is the repository of a collective unconscious. But even this collective unconscious is quite different from what Lévi-Strauss might mean by the collective and unconscious basis of myths because for Jung the latter is *genetically* determined and hence, in Lévi-Strauss' use of the term, *natural*.

Lévi-Strauss' approach to myths presents them as thoroughly Durkheimian in so far that mythemes, being arbitrary like phonemes are seen to rely on some consensus and custom for their meaning both to the peoples concerned and to anthropologist since it is only by reference to other aspects of culture and social structure that we, as outside observers, can understand them. If Lévi-Strauss denies any independent philosophical, moral, scientific, metaphysical or aesthetic reality to myths as he does, and if he insists that the *sense* of myths (understood as that which they signify) is *social*, then we might be justified in calling his approach sociocentric as well. This stress on the central importance of the social in understanding the significance of myths is the theoretical remnant in Lévi-Strauss of what was a religious cult for Comte and a socio-metaphysical conundrum for Durkheim – society understood as a *whole*.

Reductio ad absurdum

Lévi-Strauss' definition of the social as the arbitrary boils down to much the same sort of statement that we saw Durkheim and Mauss making on the last page of their *Primitive Classification*, when they had to say that if asked what was the origin of the social categories from which they imagined all other categories to be derived then one could only reply that it was 'refractory to analysis' and 'defies critical and rational examination'. If something is arbitrary then it cannot be analysed any further and does defy critical and rational examination. Supposing that we grant the unlikely proposition that the colour of traffic-lights is an arbitrary system of signs and alleged that 'Stop' might just as easily have been green, 'Go' yellow, and the intermediate signal red. It follows that it is, in that case, quite absurd to start arguing about *why* red was in fact chosen for 'Stop' in preference to green or yellow since we have already conceded that there was no reason – it was arbitrary. And if these colours really are arbitrary then critical examination of them – would 'Go' be better represented by red? – is quite inappropriate, since if all such signs are arbitrary, each is as good as any other and things are much the same in the end whatever arrangement is chosen. One might as well say '*pomme*' as say 'apple', and of course the French do.

The mention of the linguistic analogy here, always so important to Lévi-Strauss' thinking, is worth pursuing. Of course, de Saussure was correct when he maintained that the linguistic sign, in this case the word 'apple', was arbitrary in that quite incontrovertibly some people do say '*pomme*'. But this is not to say that the words '*pomme*' and 'apple' are wholly unmotivated and gratuitous. De Saussure's argument was, as we saw, that the linguistic sign is un-motivated, or arbitrary, relative to that which it signifies. Historically speaking, of course, the word '*pomme*' is not arbitrary – it is necessary if one is French. De Saussure's point is that, history and tradition apart, it is not necessary if we want to re-present the idea *apple*, that in this respect any word would, in principle, do.

I have no wish to become involved in purely linguistic arguments about the general validity or otherwise of de Saussure's principle. Suffice it to say that many see the insistence of structural linguistics that meaning (the signified) should not be taken into account in phonetics as a major weakness. It is certainly true that, as a mode of linguistic analysis, the structural linguistics of de Saussure appears not to have been able to advance beyond the relatively low level of analysis represented by phonetics and appears to be more or less wholly limited to this field.

In Lévi-Strauss' use of this idea, however, we are fully entitled, indeed obliged, to pursue this point further if we really wish to arrive at a critical understanding of what he is or is not saying.

We have already seen that the insistence on the arbitrariness of culture can easily lead to a most unsatisfactory conclusion, and I shall have more to say about just how unsatisfactory it is in a moment. Let us recall, however, that in his analysis of the origins of culture (defined as that which is arbitrary as opposed to necessary) Lévi-Strauss was certainly not saying that the avoidance of incest was completely arbitrary in the sense of being ultimately meaningless and inexplicable. In fact, for Lévi-Strauss, as we saw, the creation of culture is also the creation of the ultimate in meaning, if by meaning we mean the content, the inner subjective experience to which those cultural codes give rise. As structures, kinship systems are arbitrary in that they could structurally have been otherwise than they were, just as 'apple' is arbitrary because one could have said '*pomme*'. But we have already seen that, dialectically speaking, and seeing the situation from the point of view of the diachronic and historical evolution, kinship systems or totemic social structures are not at all arbitrary but necessary. Like words, Lévi-Strauss visualizes their link with the signified as being arbitrary, but not that which joins them to other such systems of signs, just as we saw that historically and etymologically speaking a Frenchman is not really at liberty not to say '*pomme*'.

In summary, then, we can say that cultural codes are only finally arbitrary *in the synchronic*. In the diachronic they are determined by the materialistic dialectic and therefore necessary. But structural anthropology is a science of structures and obeying the uncertainty principle cannot pretend to study structure *and* content. Hence, because a part of the content of our own society and of our own dialectic, it resigns itself to studying only the structures of other societies, of analysing them, in other words, only in the synchronic. In this dimension structural anthropology gives us knowledge *of*, not knowledge *for*. A critical understanding, as opposed to the awareness of gratuitous arbitrariness which we in fact get from it, is found only in content and never in form. Lévi-Strauss' ultimate conclusion concerning the epistemological status of our knowledge about primitive societies is thus exactly like that of Durkheim and Mauss.

But let us look at this more closely for a moment. Did we not agree that arbitrariness belonged only to the synchronic in this respect? Might not genuinely intelligible explanations be possible in the diachronic? In other words, in a *historical* anthropology rather than a structural one?

This is perfectly true. But two points need to be made in reply. The first is that, as we have seen, the uncertainty principle denies us diachronic *and* synchronic, sense *and* nonsense. Secondly, even the real understanding of content which it does allow us, for instance of our own society, is only in terms of the Marxist notion

D

of knowledge which equates knowing with *being involved in*. Marxists, like structuralists, are ultimately anti-rationalists in that they deny our capacity for independent and detached thought. If truth cannot be objective, but must always be ideological or determined by something else, whether *conscience collective* or materialistic dialectic, truth is always closer to what the simpleminded (with whom I unreservedly identify myself) would call error. For, as I argued in my chapter on Marx and Lévi-Strauss, to accord an independent, detached and genuinely critical rôle to the intelligence would be to undo the basic dogmas of dialectical materialism and open the way to a return to Comtean positivism, or at least to a sort of sociology which did not accord a primary rôle to the collective, or to history, or the dialectic etc etc. The suspension of rational criticism so clearly seen in Marxist political régimes actually originates in the sociological analysis of Marx and means that, even considered from the diachronic point of view, the ultimate explanations of social reality must appear more or less totally arbitrary. They are not arbitrary in this case because unmotivated but because they are determined by factors beyond the scope or rational criticism considered as an independent and objective undertaking.

This reduction to final arbitrariness, however, does not merely affect the analysis of culture as a social phenomenon. It also extends to the idea of nature.

We have already seen the use Lévi-Strauss makes of the idea of nature as the fundamental explanatory basis of culture. Nature, in the sense in which Lévi-Strauss uses the term, has two main meanings. First, it means the phenomenal world as we perceive it, excluding culture. In other words, nature is everything outside culture. Secondly, nature is used in the sense of 'human nature' particularly in his developments of Durkheim's mode of sociological explanation and in the final and apparently reductive explanations of totemism and myth, and indeed of culture as a whole. This human nature is what *The Savage Mind* is purportedly all about. The human nature to which cultural codes reduce and on which they are based is ultimately the nature of the mind itself.

We have already looked at some of the senses in which Lévi-Strauss understands the word 'mind'. To Anglo-Saxon readers it might seem that Lévi-Strauss were some sort of Neo-Platonist or

Idealist who, a bit like the thirteenth-century Catalan philosopher and saint, Bl. Ramón Lull, believed that all systems of philosophy, and what is more important, all religious dogmas, could be reduced to a few simple logical operations of the mind, and that once this was demonstrated to people – even infidels – it would become clear just what these fundamental logical categories or final truths might be. Ramón Lull, who was even more dogmatic in this respect than Lévi-Strauss, and understandably so, only resembles him in his belief in an abstract logic of the mind. But Lévi-Strauss, as we have already seen, is not really a crypto-Idealist at all. For him mind and nature are ultimately one. Both are natural parts of reality, and if there is final truth in the mind in the sense of there being an accurate picture of reality then this is only because the mind itself is a real and material object. This is not in any sense a species of Transcendental Idealism as some have alleged; in fact it is more a Transcendental Materialism.

This reciprocal relation between nature in the mind, and nature outside the mind, links the two uses of the word which I pointed out above. The mind ultimately reduces to nature because Lévi-Strauss sees it as a natural object, but we must notice that, the hoped-for reduction to brain-physiology apart, this 'mind' of which Lévi-Strauss speaks is fundamentally *structural*. Lévi-Strauss' unconscious is not at all like that of Freud. It is a purely structural, formal unconscious, something which structures phenomena but does not fill them in the sense of giving them content. The savage mind, as Lévi-Strauss labours to show in the book of that title, is a structuring and classifying agency. It is not what Freud might have meant by that term – a mind full of primitive instincts.

Summarizing the position, we can say that for Lévi-Strauss explanation ultimately reduces culture to nature in the sense that it traces all causal chains either to the external world of nature (which includes the materialist dialectic) or to the inner, psychological nature of the mind. This mind, as we have seen, exhibits itself in the constitution of the codes which we call culture. Culture is by definition an arbitrary structuring of arbitrary signs and reflects not the positive content of the mind (if it did culture would be nature – i.e. necessity) but rather its *form*. Outer, material reality however determines the content and meaning of these codes by a Marxist materialistic determinism. This dialectic is ultimately as inscrutable as the mind itself since knowledge is, by Marxist definiton, determined by it and not competent to function independently of it.

The difficulty associated with Lévi-Strauss' position, like that of Durkheim and Mauss, not to mention Marx and Comte who exhibit the same symptoms in a different way, is that of failing to provide a genuinely *reductive* explanation. We have just seen how the apparent reduction of the mind to brain-circuitry results in exactly the same sort of blind alley that we saw Lévi-Strauss led into by his emphasis on the arbitrary nature of cultural codes. In both cases, because content or substance was denied to the unconscious – since the sign had to be arbitrary in one case and since the mind was a purely formal entity in the other – and because the unconscious was emptied of everything except structure a reduction to some other level of reality seemed impossible. Those who argue that structuralism leads to an infinite regress of structural explanations are wrong. Structuralist explanations as found in Lévi-Strauss do not lead everywhere, in fact they lead absolutely nowhere because ultimately the mind and the systems of signs which it creates are arbitrary – that is, devoid of meaning in final terms. They are not devoid of meaning, it is true, with regard to other arbitrary realities, that is, to the rest of culture, but what I have tried to show is that Lévi-Strauss' equivalent of Durkheim's *conscience collective* is as irreducible, inexplicable and thoroughly quasi-metaphysical as anything that we have found in the work of his great predecessor. The proffered solutions to Durkheim's explanatory difficulties turn out to be not so much solutions as evasions, explanatory ploys which resolve the particular difficulty only to put another, and closely analogous one in its place. Where Durkheim and Mauss came to the end of the road with a collective emotion, Lévi-Strauss comes just as totally to a halt with the savage mind and its creation, culture.

As a matter of fact, this is hardly a criticism of Lévi-Strauss. It is much more one of the social sciences in general, because, as I pointed out at the beginning, once Comte had invented the science and handed over to it the collective aspects of human life then it was inevitable that the central issue of structuralism on which we are now touching, an issue which was equally at the core of Durkheim's paradoxes, namely that of psychological reduction, should haunt sociological theory for ever after.

This issue was present, implicitly at least, in the very name which the new science received. Comte, in doing violence to accepted grammatical practice in joining a Latin suffix to a Greek termination, already meant to imply that his brain-child would be the science of society. Now society is an abstraction. Usually, any particular society is identified with a geographical and frequently political and linguistic entity. In modern times it comes more and more to be equated with the state. Yet it is more of an abstract entity than the state and cannot be so easily defined. Everyone is meant to know what phrases like 'English society' mean, but reflection shows that the specific denotations of such terms is far from easy. Terms like 'state' or 'kingdom' or 'country' are much more easily intelligible because they contain, within them so to speak, the means of their own definition. 'Country' is clearly a geographical term. 'Kingdom' and 'state' are terms with a clear political basis. But what is the basis of the term 'society'? Presumably neither geographical nor political, but sociological. And so we are back where we began.

However, there is a second and perhaps more serious difficulty implicit in the term 'sociology'. It seems to suggest that sociology is a discipline distinct from, shall we say, history. Now historians have always studied societies, some of them with comparative and analytical methods remarkably like those of so-called 'sociologists'. Clearly, Comte did not mean that his sociologists were to be a new breed of historians. Historians study the past; the term carries with it, if I may use structuralist jargon for a moment, a strong diachronic connotation. 'Sociology', on the other hand, has an equally strong synchronic connotation. It suggests that sociologists are not historians because they are not really interested in the past. If not interested in the past, then they must be interested in the present and hence, taken along with the concentration of the discipline on 'society' as an abstract structure sociology was predestined by Comte to be the non-historical study of an abstract entity which historians had always traditionally studied in the past, but which sociology was only competent to deal with in the present, and perhaps even in the future.

This tendency then to see society as an abstract structure transcending reality and maintaining itself in the present – holistic functionalism, in other words – was contained within the very baptismal solecism which was sociology's name. It should come as little surprise to us then to see that the theoretical cul-de-sac into which Lévi-Strauss' structuralism leads us is in reality only another set of logical permutations of the same theoretical paradoxes – that sociology studies a reality which is abstract, and that it explains a self-maintaining whole which is always changing and which is only composed of individual parts. There exist only two ways of escape from these difficulties, both of which imply abandoning sociology altogether. One possibility is to become a historian and so overcome the synchronic prejudice of sociology; the other is to become a psychologist and so dissolve the abstraction which only sociologists claim to be able to understand – society – back into its component parts – human beings.

Complete psychological reductionism thus is, and must remain, anathema to most sociologists because, as a methodological and theoretical approach, it threatens to replace their science altogether and to demote it to being a department of psychology. Lévi-Strauss and Durkheim may well both be highly psychological in their approach to social phenomena, but neither, as we have seen, would go all the way and reduce the social and collective to the psychological and individual. But what might be a virtue in the eyes of sociologists anxious to defend their beleaguered subject from the attacks of other disciplines might appear, to one more concerned with the final explanatory value of the sociological approach, a grave error, if not a real intellectual vice. The alternative, horrified sociologists will probably believe, must be some kind of psychoanalytic or behaviourist approach to social phenomena – an approach which seeks to reduce all collective phenomena to terms of individual psychology. It is my contention that Lévi-Strauss' structuralism can be shown to be a modified version of just such a reductionist mode of explanation, and that it is in reality little more than a form of psychoanalysis which has not, however, been allowed to reduce to realities – that is, man's physical and instinctual nature.

A footnote to Freud

Where Lévi-Strauss' explanations do reduce to nature, that nature is, as we have seen, little more than an abstract idea; where they reduce to culture, that culture is essentially arbitrary. Its arbitrariness arises out of the fact that it is the product of collective consciousness which Lévi-Strauss, like Durkheim and Mauss in their *Primitive Classification*, was unable to reduce to anything very intelligible. This unintelligibility of the final terms of the Lévi-Straussian system is by far the most damaging criticism that one can make of it.

But if culture were not arbitrary, if the link between sign and signified were motivated, then the great break which Lévi-Strauss introduces between nature and culture would not exist. Culture would be seen as the outcome of man's individual instinctual and non-social self, and cultural codes like kinship and cooking would be seen as motivated by deep instinctual and psychological currents. The result would be something indistinguishable from the approach of Freud.

If we compare Lévi-Strauss' writings with those of Freud one or two remarkable similarities emerge, similarities which suggest that Lévi-Strauss owes more to Freud than to any other writer so far mentioned in these pages. *Elementary Structures of Kinship*, *Totemism* and *The Savage Mind* all bear a very close and striking similarity to Freud's *Totem and Taboo*, and his huge *Mythologiques* seems essentially to be *The Interpretation of Dreams* recast in a structuralist mode.

Let us take *Totem and Taboo* first. Freud argues that totemism is characterized by a ritual worship of a tabooed totem (usually an animal) and by a system of exogamous clans. The aim of these clans is to prevent the infringement of the laws prohibiting incest, and the totem for Freud is a collective animal phobia which represents the primal father against whom the sons revolted because of his total domination of the 'mothers'. Totemism is therefore a close parallel in group psychology to the animal phobias found commonly among young children. The rule of exogamy is the collective equivalent of the individual incest prohibitions which underlie the nuclear family. The institution of totemism as a historical event represents a transition from savagery to culture because it involves repression and sublimation of basic instincts and the setting up of social means to further these and provide symbolic representation of the repressed and now renounced incestuous wishes. The sons who revolted against the father institute incest-avoidance as a means of eliminating the very Oedipal conflicts which led them to overthrow him in the first place. But along with this they also enthrone the rejected father as the superego in the guise of the animal totem, surrounded by all the ambivalence which Freud identifies with the word 'taboo'.

Lévi-Strauss' argument in *Elementary Structures of Kinship* is an inverted version of this. Freud, as we saw, argued that the whole point of totemism and exogamy was that of avoiding incestuous relations and their associated Oedipal conflicts. The prohibition of incest, the beginnings of human culture, arise out of the fraternal desire of the triumphant sons not to get themselves into the same position as their now eradicated father, particularly with regard to their own sons. Renunciation, repression and sublimation are the means by which these incestuous wishes are dealt with. Art, magic, religion and social organization are the results.

But according to Lévi-Strauss exogamy exists not because men desire to avoid incest, but rather because men need to exchange sisters. The transition from nature to culture comes about for man-kind when men forgo their own women and exchange them for those of other groups. The result is a system of 'signs' from which political and kinship ties result which provide a social infrastructure upon which other systems of communication, such as those of words, goods and services and so on, can be established. In other words, Lévi-Strauss analyses exogamy in terms of its function for the social structure. Incest-avoidance is the means by which the end of exogamy, actually based on the idea of sister-exchange, is realized in practice.

We have already seen that this is a thinly disguised Rous-seauesque social contract. Man gives up the State of Nature – which means incest but also isolation – for reciprocating kinship ties and social contacts with other men. But clearly, it is also what Freud might have termed an *overdetermined* theory of exogamy, since it is perfectly compatible with the argument of *Totem and Taboo*, and represents a sociological, conscious and functional determining cause as opposed to the psychological, unconscious and historical causes discussed by Freud.

If we leave totemism for a moment and turn to a consideration of *Mythologiques* in the light of *The Interpretation of Dreams*, we shall once again see a very clear parallel between the approaches of Freud and Lévi-Strauss.

In the table on page 105 I have set out, on the top line, the basic anecdotic units of the Oedipus myth. Read from left to right these represent the simplest possible version of the story and correspond to the way in which we saw Lévi-Strauss presenting some myths in chapter 2. This is not the only representation of the Oedipus myth

Oedipus	Prophesied that Oedipus will kill his father		left to die by father	The question which should not be answered, but is (riddle of Sphinx)
Parsifal	Prophesied that Parsifal will redeem his adoptive father, Amfortas	when he has found the spear	leaves his mother to die	The question which should be asked, but is not
Lohengrin	Prophesied that Lohengrin will redeem Elsa		Elsa left an orphan	The question which should not be asked, but is
Ring	Wotan prophesies that Seigfried will kill his step-father, Mime	when he has made the sword	leaves his step-father and kills him	

Oedipus	Oedipus marries his mother because he does not recognize her	Oedipus damns himself and his mother, kills his father	Oedipus blinds himself, ends wise but tainted
Parsifal	Parsifal remains chaste because he remembers his adoptive father	Parsifal redeems himself, a mother surrogate, Kundry, and cures his adoptive father	Parsifal's 'eyes are opened' begins foolish but pure
Lohengrin	Lohengrin marries Elsa on condition that he remains unrecognized	Elsa damns herself, but her brother is redeemed	
Ring	Siegmund dies because he recognizes his sister and marries her	Siegmund is destroyed but his sister is saved	
	Siegfried dies because he does not recognize his half-sister, Brunhilde, and divorces her	Siegfried kills his step-father, is himself destroyed, but his half-sister, Brunhilde, redeems the world through destruction of her father, Wotan	

that can be obtained in this way. Lévi-Strauss, in his *Structural Anthropology* for instance, suggests a different one. Nevertheless, a comparison of the way I have presented it here with Lévi-Strauss' methods in *Mythologiques* will show that this analysis is faithful to his structural principles. Beneath the Oedipus myth, and providing in musicological terms its 'counterpoint', I have set out the Parsifal myth as found in Wagner's music-drama. In doing so I have followed a number of hints made by Lévi-Strauss, principally in his lecture *The Scope of Anthropology*.

Because the signs constituting the myths are purely structural and their logical relations the only meaning that they can carry, it follows that a logically inverted version of the Oedipus myth is just as possible as a musically inverted version of, shall we say, the theme in Bach's *Art of Fugue*. The logical kinship linking music and myth means that although both use different systems of significant units, both are structurally very similar and hence the tabular representation of the myths which I have presented is a 'score' in which the 'melody' – the story – reads diachronically from left to right, and the 'harmony' – the logical contrasts – reads synchronically up and down. Hence the question motive in Oedipus (the riddle of the Sphinx) – a question which should not be answered, but is – is the exact opposite of the situation which we find as the most important element in the Parsifal legend – namely, a question which should be asked (Parsifal's to the wounded King), but is not. Just as the answering of the riddle of the Sphinx leads Oedipus straight to disaster, so the failure to ask the question (whose asking it had been prophesied would cure the King) leads Parsifal into a situation where he suddenly comes to his senses and redeems himself.

Again, I have suggested in the table that another structural permutation of the same idea can be found in Wagner's *Lohengrin*, where again a question if of central importance in the unfolding of the drama. Hence in the Lohengrin legend, we find a question which should not be asked, but is – that of Elsa enquiring Lohengrin's name and lineage – and which is in different ways a logical reversal of the question element in both Oedipus and Parsifal.

The reader will have noticed that the structural analysis of these myths and the anecdotic table which I have provided are exactly like those which I reproduced from Lévi-Strauss' *Mythologiques* on page 59 above. He may also notice, looking back, that there is something highly Freudian about the myths in question. Indeed, they appear to be a striking example of the well-known psychoanalytic identification of both snakes and wild carnivores with the penis. The reader will not, I hope, feel that I have been partial or unfair in my choice of these three myths. If he cares to look at random through the pages of *Mythologiques* he will find that nearly all the myths appear to have been recounted by someone well acquainted with the more abstruse aspects of the psychoanalytical theory of dream symbolism. Volume one of *Mythologiques*, *The Raw and the Cooked*, begins with the 'myth of reference' which is all about incest and copulation/castration (hero's buttocks gnawed off by birds etc). Volume two, *From Honey to Ashes*, begins with a series of myths illustrating the anal-sadistic theme of the equivalence of food and excrement. *The Origin of Table Manners*, volume three, begins with the identification of the 'heavenly bodies' with the parts of all-too-human bodies in a way which is familar to us from the literature of psychoanalysis.

The reader will have guessed that I chose the Oedipus myth as the principal 'melody' of this polyphony of myths for ulterior reasons. These were the desire to contrast as starkly as possible the Lévi-Straussian and Freudian approaches to the phenomenon in question. For Lévi-Strauss, as we have seen, the myths set out in the table are structural variations on one theme whose ultimate significance, as he suggests in his analysis of the Oedipus myth in *Structural Anthropology*, is to resolve logical contradictions arising out of what we have seen to be the basic opposition, that between nature and culture.

Freud would, I believe, have been quite happy with the tabular analysis which I have presented. The structural inversion of the Oedipus myth with regard to that of Parsifal is exactly what one would expect from his analysis of dreams and hysterical symptoms. Indeed, in his *Interpretation of Dreams*[1] Freud points out the importance of precisely this sort of logical inversion:

. . . reversal, or turning a thing into its opposite, is one of the means of representation most favoured by the dream-work, and one which is capable of employment in the most diverse directions.

But the analogy at the back of Freud's mind is always that which compares dreams or myths with literature rather than music. Freud is not interested in the structural properties of myths to the extent that we have seen Lévi-Strauss to be. Consequently, it is not surprising that he would not share the French anthropologist's notion about the deep similarity linking myth to music. For Freud, structural processes, such as that of logical reversal, are interesting merely as revealing the means which the mind employs to realize certain ends. In the case of dreams and the collective fantasies which we call myths these ends are the expression of repressed and latent thoughts in a distorted manifest content. The analysis of myths and dreams for Freud was like the deciphering of some strange text written in unknown characters. The puzzling inscription corresponds to the manifest content of the dream or myth, usually, as in the case of most of the myths in *Mythologiques*, quite beyond the pale of commonsense. The process of translation corresponds to that of un-covering the underlying latent thoughts which are invariably far from unintelligible. In the case of the myths which we have been considering it is quite obvious that Freud would regard the Parsifal myth as precisely one of those reversals which he came to expect from the analysis of dreams. The Lohengrin and *Ring* examples, which again show frequent incidents of hidden identities, incestuous liasons, questions and answers, would be treated by Freud as other possible distortions of the basic Oedipus myth, which is itself based on the latent and repressed desires of humans to commit incest and to undo the creation of civilization which he theorized about in the pages of *Totem and Taboo*.

But here again, Freud and Lévi-Strauss, although apparently op-posed in their attitude to myths, are in fact very close. As we saw, in the last analysis myth for Lévi-Strauss is a question of reconciling the contradictions between nature and culture and, like totemism, cooking, kinship and a thousand other things, reflects the basic interplay of nature and culture in the world. But for Freud the dream and the myth fulfil exactly the same rôle, if by nature we mean the id, the animal, the material and the repressed, and if by culture we mean the superego, the moral law, the human and the spiritual. Both are determinists who see nature – Lévi-Strauss as an abstract idea, Freud as the unconscious and instinctual – as pro-viding determining causes to which their respective explanations reduce.

These observations also apply to the subject of totemism. For Lévi-Strauss, nature plays a pre-eminent rôle in totemism, indeed it plays two rôles. First as the system of signs used by the language of totemism to represent and to define social groups, and secondly as the basis of the unconscious ordering processes of the mind which classify nature and culture in the same way to produce a homologous series of categories. But, here again, Freud's theory is in fact closer to Lévi-Strauss than would appear superficially – a point particularly important since to many Lévi-Strauss' explanations of totemism in *The Savage Mind* appear most typical of his whole methodology and completely representative of structuralism in anthropology.

Freud's collective animal phobia also puts nature in a leading rôle – the animal species symbolizes the overthrown father, or, in other words, the superego. But the superego plays in Freud's social psychology a part analogous to that of the totemic language in Lévi-Strauss' pseudo-linguistic analysis. The superego represents society for Freud, it is the repository of collective values, especially in the case of totemism where it symbolizes and enshrines the pre-eminent moral prohibition against incest. The group, in this case the totemic clan, is the group because of its shared superego, the totem, the representation of the primal father. Expressed in the language of dream analysis, one could say that the totem is the naturalistically distorted manifest content of a system of social symbolism whose aim is the prohibition of incest and the maintenance of the identity of inter-marrying clans. Expressed in these terms Freud's theory is identical to that of Lévi-Strauss, except that where Freud has a symbolic system, Lévi-Strauss would have a language – assuming the latter to connote arbitrary significant units.

This brings us to the heart of the matter of the similarities between these two analysts of the mind. Where in the theory of psychoanalysis we find a latent *content* ultimately depending on the instincts, in Lévi-Strauss' structuralism we find an unconscious *structure* which, in the last analysis, is determined by the logic of nature written into the circuitry of the brain. Thus, inevitably, Lévi-Strauss rejects the notion of a symbolism of latent meanings in favour of a language of deep structures. The mind is emptied of all content which is not in the first place the outcome of such structures. Myths are memorable because ultimately the mind is musical.

A number of writers, such as H. Stewart Hughes in his *The Obstructed Path*, have pointed out the tendency of French intellectuals to de-sexualize psychoanalysis wherever they come into contact with it. Lévi-Strauss' structuralism is just such a hygenically de-libidinized version of Freudianism.

Both Freud and Lévi-Strauss start with a belief in the primacy of the unconscious, but where one makes this unconscious individualistic and irrational, the other makes it collective and rational and appears to substitute for the libido of Freud the *cogito* of Descartes. Where for Freud there is first and foremost the body with its instincts, there for Lévi-Strauss is the mind. It is a mind which reflects and is created by nature sure enough, just as in myths and totemism it is in its turn reflected in nature. Yet this nature on which it rests is for Lévi-Strauss little more than an abstract principle. Indeed, one can hardly help remembering that in Freud's view such a philosophical and abstract notion of the natural would appear to give it all the characteristics of the ideal and cultural.

Structuralism and cybernetics

However, I do not believe that it would be at all fitting or adequate to end a study of Lévi-Strauss' structuralism with the assertion that what was wrong with it was that it was French and consequently mysteriously impervious to the revelations of psychoanalysis. Clearly this is not enough. What must be accounted for is the particular transformation which the ideas of Freud have undergone at his hands. To say that the French have a particular aversion for the barbarisms of psychoanalysis – that is, the libido theory – may well be true, regarding the French as we must as the most civilized people of Europe, but on its own this explanation does not go far enough.

If we follow Lévi-Strauss' lead and regard his structuralism as a myth, then we may approach this question by asking why the myth is the way it is. The only difficulty here is that a structuralist approach to the structuralist myth will not take us very far, structuralism being the very thing which we wish to analyse. A structural analysis of structuralism is, as I remarked in my preface, a pretty tautological undertaking, and one which has already been repeated often enough to make another attempt at it quite undesirable. For my part – and at this point the author must finally show his hand – I prefer a psychoanalytical approach to the structuralist myth.

Myths like structuralism are collective fantasies. These fantasies are basically comparable to dreams, whose laws of formation and functioning they obey. The myth is thus a wish-fulfilment which works out unconscious latent thoughts under the distorting and deceiving cover of a manifest content. Now the latent content of Lévi-Strauss' structuralism I have already discussed. It is, as we saw, a de-libidinized Freudianism, a Cartesian psychoanalysis. What remains to be explained then is not the latent content, which I hope stands revealed, or even the wish-fulfilment, which is obviously that of a denial of the libido (that is, its repression, one of the most common of all wish-fulfilments), but rather the superficial aspects of structuralism, the *manifest content*.

Norbert Wiener, in the first chapter of his epoch-making book *Cybernetics*, points out that, since about 1700, each century has been dominated by one particular scientific revolution and by technological, economic and ideological forms associated with it. In the case of the eighteenth century, the scientific revolution was that of Newtonian physics. The technological innovation corresponding to this was the pendulum clock, based as it was on the laws of motion; and the ideological revolution which went with it was mercantilism – the development of accurate sea-going chronometers having been of the first importance in the development of eighteenth-century trade.

If the eighteenth century was the great age of Newtonian mechanics, then the nineteenth century was that of classical thermodynamics, and the scientists which we associate with it, men like Carnot, Boltzmann and Joule, all made significant contributions to the new science. Technologically, it was the age of the great thermodynamic machines, the steam-engine, whose impact was so far-reaching and which did for nineteenth-century trade and industry what the chronometer had done for that of the eighteenth. Ideologically the nineteenth century, the age of statistical thermodynamics, saw the birth of 'statistical' philosophies and the concern for the average man evidenced in the rise of socialism and the revolutions of 1830 and 1848.

The twentieth century, according to Wiener, is the age of cybernetics, defined as the science of communication and control in animals and machines. Its greatest technological development is the computer. The computer is to the twentieth century what the steam-engine was to the nineteenth and the clock mechanism was to the eighteenth. From the economic point of view, one need only reflect for a moment on the tremendous impact of computers and computerization on modern business and defence. Ideologically speaking, it seems to me that nothing corresponds more closely to the cybernetic revolution in science than structuralism. Indeed, Lévi-Strauss himself admits structuralism in the social sciences to be only a small part of a larger and more general science of communication, itself one of the two major aspects of Wiener's cybernetics.

In myths or collective fantasies, as in dreams, the manifest content has a crucial function to fulfil. In the case of structuralism, the cybernetic aspects which manifest themselves in an overwhelming emphasis on systems of communication (hence huge borrowings from structural linguistics), and in the tendency to treat the mind as if it were a computer or logic machine results in the latent content – de-sexualized psychoanalysis – being presented in a way which makes it highly acceptable by virtue of its close proximity, ideologically speaking, to a branch of modern science which is new, prestigious, and politically and economically of the first importance. It also has a second useful function in that the desire to treat the mind like a cybernetic mechanism furthers the unconscious wish-fulfilment in that it easily allows a complete divorce to be established between mind and body, and appears to rule out of account physical realities like instincts and unconscious drives. The more logical and structural the mind can be shown to be, the more it resembles the technological wonder of modern times – the computer.

The ecumenical anthropologist

Structuralism may be the most obvious example of contemporary sociological thought borrowing the trappings of cybernetics for its own purposes, but it is not the only one. Talcott Parsons also owes something to the new science of cybernetics, but in his case what he owes is of a more fundamental nature. Indeed, one could go further and say that all twentieth-century sociology is deeply in harmony with the cybernetic viewpoint in just the same way that, following Wiener, I suggested that eighteenth-century mercantilism or nineteenth-century socialism could be seen to be in harmony with the scientific revolutions of those years. In discussing the problem of reduction in sociological explanation I pointed out that, in wishing to be something different from the historian or the psychologist, the sociologist had to emphasize the collective and synchronic aspects of his subject. This led him to invent the idea of an abstract entity called 'society' and to come to see it as a largely self-maintaining and functional whole, irreducile to its parts – human beings – or to its past – history. In the first half of this century this attitude to society found inspiration in what is known as the 'organismic analogy'. This was the use of the idea, taken from biology, of self-regulating and homeostatic biological entities which behaved in a way clearly explicable by the functionalist theory. We have already seen that Durkheim's sociocentric theory of society is almost indistinguishable from this. It was, as we saw, an approach to society which saw it mainly in terms of the synchronic, of self-maintenance, and which explained social institutions in terms of how they contributed to the persistence of the social whole. However, after 1950 and the emergence of cybernetics as a science of communication and control, it became clear that the cybernetic notion of self-regulation, and in particular the idea of negative feed-back mechanisms, was even more pertinent to sociology than the biological, organismic idea. The latter had in fact been the most obvious and commonly met with example of the former. Biological organisms are constructed as self-maintaining mechanisms on cybernetic principles and what Wiener's new science did was to enable us to generalize and quantify the communication and control systems underlying all self-regulating processes. No wonder then that Parsons took up the idea and applied overtly cybernetic notions to society. Doubtless Durkheim would have done the same thing if he had lived a half-century later.

The emphasis on the collective as opposed to the individual and on the present as opposed to the past is the essence of modern sociology. It leads, as we have just seen, to an intrinsically cybernetic outlook on social phenomena. Lévi-Strauss, as a twentieth-century and not a nineneteenth-century sociologist, is deeply affected by this, more so than he is by the Marxist approach which is the equivalent of the statistical and thermodynamic revolution in scientific thought in the last century. Consequently the basis of his sociology is functionalistic, as was that of Durkheim and as is that of Talcott Parsons. His analysis of kinship is basically functionalistic in that he explains kinship systems in terms of the control and communication of women between groups of men. The key explanatory idea, the avoidance of incest, is introduced from Freud to show how it results in a positive social function – that of creating reciprocating kinship links between otherwise isolated persons. Totemism is analysed in terms of its function for communication and control within the social group – that of defining it and creating a language in which to express it. Every other social code he isolates is explained in the same way and in *Mythologiques* his great analysis of myth brings him close to the conclusions of Parsons in *The Social System* in that both seem to conclude that the psychological basis of society is a vast interlocking system of mutually supporting ideas.

But contemporary sociology is not merely cybernetic in inspiration, it is, as I argued at the beginning of this book, scholastic in temperament. I showed how the writings of Talcott Parsons could be compared with those of Sartre and how both could be seen as synthetic, post-classical writers interested in the production of didactic compendia of sociology. Much the same could be said of the late works of Weber and Pareto (who otherwise unquestionably belonged to the classical phase), and of other less important modern sociologists like Merton, Shutz and perhaps even Gouldner. All of these sociologists manifest to a greater or lesser degree the characteristics of scholasticism – academicism, dependence on classical theories, a desire for synthesis and for systematic explanation, use of jargon only intelligible to initiates, pedagogic concerns, and so on.

Lévi-Strauss' sociology is less unlike these scholastic efforts than it may appear to be on the surface. In having alluded to the common quasi-cybernetic basis of both Parsons' and Lévi-Strauss' sociologies and in pointing out the similarities between Talcott Parsons and Sartre and the significance of the latter for Lévi-Strauss I have already given some cause for suspecting that he may be much more closely related to the main stream of modern sociology than many may appreciate. But if Talcott Parsons' scholasticism is synthetic, then Lévi-Strauss' approach is what I would call 'ecumenical'. An elucidation of this point will constitute an excellent excuse to summarize the findings of our survey of his theoretical sociology.

If we look at the first issue which we considered, which we might for convenience call Durkheim's first paradox, we shall recall that it concerned the historical origin of the social fact. The paradox can be explained as follows: Society is composed of a collective consciousness. This collective consciousness is transmitted by socialization, and socialization is transmitted by the collective consciousness. Yet the collective consciousness must have had a beginning.

Lévi-Strauss resolved this paradox by recourse to a Rousseauesque theory of a structural social contract in which men began to exchange sisters and to avoid incest for reasons ultimately reducible to natural causes. Here the fundamental problem, the derivation of culture from nature, is solved by use of de Saussure's notion of the arbitrary nature of the linguistic sign which Lévi-Strauss extended to all collective representations. The fundamental contradiction which Lévi-Strauss insists all myths finally reduce to is that existing between nature and culture, a contradiction which his own structural 'myths' can also be seen as an attempt to solve.

Durkheim's second paradox was logically related to the first. The reader will doubtless recall that it runs something as follows: All individual thought is derived from the collective consciousness. Yet the collective consciousness exists only in individual minds. Yet the collective consciousness cannot be reduced to the content of individual minds.

Lévi-Strauss' solution to this, closely following that of the previous paradox, was to resort to structural linguistics for a means of escape. Here the collective aspects of the *conscience collective* were explained by reduction to a physiological uniformity among men, and the apparently inexplicable and arbitrary nature of collective representations by reference to unconscious but rational procedures of thought. Here culture was shown to reduce to nature, this time in the brain.

The third paradox said that an unchanging normative consensus was the underlying principle of the collective consciousness. Yet the collective consciousness undergoes change. Here once again structural linguistics providing the distinction between synchronic and diachronic, Code and Message, enabled Lévi-Strauss to solve the problem by showing that Durkheim's normative consensus only appertained to collective representations understood as Code, not as Message.

Finally, the fourth paradox, which states that sociology is a positive science, yet one which must take account of values both in society and the sociologist, Lévi-Strauss dealt with by defining the rôle of values to be in the diachronic and that of positivism to be in the synchronic.

In each of these cases Lévi-Strauss' approach is characterized by an ecumenical solution since, unlike Sartre or Talcott Parsons, Lévi-Strauss allows each of the reconciled elements to stand whole and largely unmodified in the plenitude of its explanatory power. Marxism is not, Lévi-Strauss would claim, compromised by Durkheimianism in his use of both of these in the solutions to the third and fourth paradoxes. In each case dialectical materialism is allowed to do what it is in fact best fitted to do, namely to explain social change in the case of the third paradox, and to define the meaning and scope of values, not to mention their exact identity, in the case of the fourth. Again, Durkheimian positivism is not, merely by being restricted to the synchronic, thereby undermined in any way. Durkheim himself was ready to admit the competence of history and other disciplines in explaining social change, and all that Lévi-Strauss need claim to have done is to have realized the true explanatory scope of Durkheimianism and formulated it in a particularly useful way.

Thus Lévi-Strauss' theoretical position contains within it, but without coercion, as it were, Durkheimian positivism as well as Marxist dialectics, Marcel Mauss as well as Ferdinand de Saussure, Roman Jakobson and Jean-Jacques Rousseau, subjective values and objective truths, systems of normative collective representations as well as dialectical, changing and contending social forces, consciousness and unconsciousness, nature and culture. A system of sociological explanation which Lévi-Strauss believes to be analogous to myth thereby becomes a body of mythical dogma, a structuralist creed. In one, whole, catholic, and certainly apostolic church, each of the great divisions of the socio-anthropological doctrine finds its place and all believers can be reconciled.

Structural anthropology, which is now at the height of its vogue, and which originated in the scholastic – which is to say in the last – era of sociological thought, needs, in order to achieve anything at all, a theoretical complexion comparable to that of the other great orthodoxy of modern sociology – Parsonianism. To achieve this it must show itself to have overcome the difficulties which prevented Durkheim from reaching final explanations and to be conformable to Marxism and the facts of modern social change. It must account for itself in terms of its own explanatory categories and be prepared to apply to itself the dogmas which it uses against all other forms of thought and systems of explanation. Finally, it must be capable of providing reductive explanations of culture and be able to resolve the last and greatest contradiction of all – the equation of culture with nature. In short, structural anthropology must be ecumenical.

Lévi-Strauss' structural analysis is at present much discussed. Its staying-power as an intellectual movement probably depends on its originality, the depth of its insight, and the breadth of its synthesis. It may survive to remain a permanent addition to human understanding, particularly in the fields of anthropology and sociology. It may again, on further reflection, come to be seen as little more than a Cartesian heresy in the history of psychoanalysis, as a quite incorrigibly French footnote to Freud.

Notes

Chapter 1

1. Auguste Comte, *The Positive Philosophy*, London 1853, p. 2.
2. Ibid., p. 3.
3. Ibid., p. 14.
4. Ibid., p. 16.
5. Auguste Comte, *Maxims*, London 1890.
6. Emile Durkheim, *The Division of Labour*, New York 1964, appendix.
7. Emile Durkheim, *Rosseau and Montesquieu*, Michigan 1960.
8. Emile Durkheim, *The Rules of Sociological Method*, Glencoe 1966, p. 21.
9. Durkheim and Mauss, *Primitive Classification*, London 1963, p. 86.
10. Ibid., p. 86.
11. Emile Durkheim, *Suicide*, New York 1951, p. 390.
12. Marcel Mauss, *The Gift*, London 1954, chapter 4.

Chapter 2

1. Edmund Leach, *Lévi-Strauss*, London 1970.
2. Durkheim and Mauss, *Primitive Classification* London 1963, p. 82.
3. Claude Lévi-Strauss, *The Savage Mind*, London 1966, p. 9.
4. Ibid., p. 11.
5. Ibid., p. 13.
6. Ibid., p. 13.
7. Ferdinand de Saussure, *Cours de linguistique genérale*, Paris 1962, p. 25, my translation.
8. Roman Jakobson in *Proceedings of the Sixth International Congress of Linguists*.
9. Jakobson and Halle, *Fundamentals of Language*, The Hague 1960, p. 45.
10. Claude Lévi-Strauss, *Structural Anthropology*, London 1968, p. 210.

11. George Steiner, 'Conversation with Lévi-Strauss', in *Encounter 26*.
12. Ferdinand de Saussure, *Cours de Linguistique genérale*, Paris 1962, p. 36, my translation.
13. Claude Lévi-Strauss, *The Raw and the Cooked*, London 1970, p. 48.
14. Ibid., pp. 99–104.

Chapter 3

1. Claude Lévi-Strauss, *The Savage Mind*, London 1966, p. 117.
2. Ibid., p. 130.
3. Ibid., p. 130.
4. Claude Lévi-Strauss, *L'homme nu (Mythologiques IV)*, Paris 1971, p. 190.

Chapter 4

1. Claude Lévi-Strauss, *The Savage Mind*, London 1966, p. 253.
2. Ibid., p. 269.
3. George Charbonnier, *Conversations with Lévi-Strauss*, London 1969, p. 33.
4. Claude Lévi-Strauss, *The Savage Mind*, London 1966, p. 254 et seq.

Chapter 5

1. Sigmund Freud, *The Interpretation of Dreams*, Standard Edition of the Complete Psychological Works of Freud, Volume IV, p. 327.

Bibliography

Some of the main sources on Lévi-Strauss' structuralism, with added comments.

R. Barthes, *Elements of Semiology* (London, 1968). A useful introduction to some of the background ideas of structuralism.

G. Charbonnier, *Conversations with C. Lévi-Strauss* (London 1969). An interesting insight into Lévi-Strauss' not-very-interesting ideas about art and culture in general.

W. Desan, *The Marxism of Jean-Paul Sartre* (New York 1965). This is an indispensable guide to Sartre's long and almost unreadable *Critique de raison dialectique*, against which Lévi-Strauss is arguing in the closing chapters of *The Savage Mind*.

M. Glucksmann, *Structuralist Analysis in Contemporary Social Thought* (London 1974). A book which is hard going, but useful in discussing Louis Althusser as well.

Hayes & Hayes, Ed., *Claude Lévi-Strauss – The Anthropologist as Hero* (Massachusetts 1970). An uneven book of essays, a few of which repay study.

M. Lane, Ed., *Structuralism – A Reader* (London 1970). The principal interest of this book is that it contains, among much irrelevant material, an essay by Lévi-Strauss and Jacobson on Baudelaire's *Les Chats*.

E. Leach, *Lévi-Strauss* (London 1970). Written very much from the point of view of British social anthropology, it contains, despite its brevity, a breathless structuralist romp through the whole of Greek mythology.

C. Lévi-Strauss, *Elementary Structures of Kinship* (London 1969). Huge and highly technical, it can only be recommended for experts or masochists.

Tristes Tropiques (London 1973). This is more of a travel book than a sociological treatise, but it does reveal Lévi-Strauss as very much the French philosopher and *litterateur*.

Totemism (London 1964). Little more than a preliminary essay to the following.

The Savage Mind (London 1966). This is a book which almost defeated the translators and which might defeat the reader on the first attempt. Second and subsequent readings show this to be Lévi-Strauss' masterpiece, whatever his structuralism does, or does not, amount to.

The Raw and the Cooked (London 1969).

From Honey to Ashes (London 1971). These are the first two volumes of Lévi-Strauss' huge *Mythologiques*, and are heavy going by any standards. Here the Freudianism of Lévi-Strauss' structuralism is only thinly disguised and shows through particularly clearly at the beginning of the second volume.

'French Sociology' in Gurvitch and Moore, Eds., *Twentieth Century Sociology, The Scope of Anthropology* (London 1968). Both of these essays reveal the extent of Lévi-Strauss' debt to Durkheim.

O. Paz, *Introduction to Lévi-Strauss* (London 1972). A completely misleading title which should read 'Introduction to O. Paz'.

Acknowledgement

Mythemes 23, 24 and 26 on pages 56–9, and the table on page 59 appear in C. Lévi-Strauss, *The Raw and the Cooked*, and are reproduced by courtesy of Jonathan Cape and Harper & Row.

Index